the Insider's Guide to ADHD

**Adults with ADHD Reveal the Secret
to Parenting Kids with ADHD**

PENNY WILLIAMS

Grace-Everett Press

Published in the United States by Grace-Everett Press

www.Grace-EverettPress.com

ISBN 978-0-9916178-5-2

Printed in the United States of America

First Edition

Foreword

Through my talents and energy, I've shared my personal story — of growing up as the "special" kid — with thousands of people around the world. That opportunity has been a blessing in my life for twenty years now.

"Special" is the word they used back in the day for those of us who were different, or not "normal." Looking back, the greatest frustration for my parents and teachers (and me!) was probably not being able to understand what was happening to me and how to best deal with it. The diagnoses of LD, ADHD, and Dyslexia were nothing but a bunch of letters that offered no clue as to what was really going on inside my head. The adults around me tried to be supportive and understanding in the most logical way they could, but it was apparent that normal logic just didn't apply to a "special" kid like me.

Today, some thirty years after my diagnosis, scientists and doctors know a lot more about learning disabilities, ADHD, and autism. Yet, parents and educators continue to struggle as they try to translate lots of new scientific data into how to constructively work with their child on a day-to-day basis. While the behavioral characteristics of ADHD are typically easy to spot, those who don't have the disorder simply cannot understand what it's like to live with it. That means even the most well-meaning adults often draw the wrong conclusions and implement the wrong strategies, simply trying to help their child.

I recently received an email from a high school student with ADHD. She was contemplating suicide because she felt "like a freak." Not one person in her life seemed to understand why she did the things she did. Those who were aware of her disorder simply treated her as if something was wrong with her. Her cry for help came in the form of a simple but profound question, "Is it just me, or can you relate to what I am going through?"

It's not enough to know the science of ADHD. It's not enough to understand the physiology of ADHD. It's not enough to know the different characteristics of an individual with ADHD. In addition to all of these, you also need to become the best possible ally your child has. That requires grasping, as closely as possible, what goes through your child's mind as they go about their days, attending school, socializing with friends, and trying to be the best son or daughter they can be.

In *The Insider's Guide to ADHD,* Penny agrees that a person without ADHD will never *fully* understand what it's like to live with ADHD. Yet, she does a great job of coaxing the reader to step into the shoes of someone who does have ADHD by sharing deeply personal stories and featuring interviews with adults who grew up with ADHD. At the heart of this immensely touching and practical book is a well-rounded discussion of what works and what doesn't for kids with ADHD. Penny offers sound strategies to help parents overcome some of the challenges of raising a child with ADHD while retaining their sanity and helping preserve their kid's self-esteem. This book will both encourage and equip you to be your child's best advocate!

Ben Glenn
The Simple ADHD Expert & The Chalk Guy
simplybenglenn.com

Intro

Are behavioral and developmental doctors, neurologists, psychologists, psychiatrists, therapists, etc. who specialize in diagnosing and/or treating ADHD really the "experts" on ADHD? They have spent an enormous amount of time studying ADHD research and working with patients. However, if you don't have ADHD yourself, how do you *really* know what it is like? You just can't. It's a way of experiencing the world that just can't be explained.

I have been obsessively studying ADHD and my son's needs, triggers, and intricacies for seven years now. *Seven* years. I am definitely an expert on my son's needs, but I still have no idea what it's like to walk around this earth with ADHD, to try to fit when you have a different perspective and a different brain.

Let me be clear right from the start, I am *not* slamming ADHD experts. To be fair, there are some ADHD experts who also have ADHD — Dr. Edward Hallowell and Terry Matlen instantly come to mind. They do really know what it's like, and their advice comes from a place of experience for sure.

Most parents don't have access to doctors and therapists who have ADHD themselves though. And, if the parent doesn't have ADHD either, then no one on the child's treatment team really, truly knows what it's like to be a child with ADHD. No one.

Not knowing my own son Ricochet's unique and challenging perspective of the world has haunted me since he was diagnosed with ADHD in November, 2008. How could I effectively help him and guide him through his challenging journey if I couldn't see his world the way he does? The answer is simply that I couldn't.

I'm a mom of ~~obsession~~ action though. I was driven to uncover this information. It was like having a perpetual itch I couldn't reach to scratch. It made me a little nutty.

And so, the idea for *The Insider's Guide to ADHD* was born. Who better to tell me what life is like for my son than the true ADHD experts, the adults who also grew up with similar challenges born of ADHD? That inside perspective was the best I was going to get, since I don't have ADHD myself.

I surveyed ninety-five adults with ADHD. I then interviewed many further to achieve a clear visual of life growing up with ADHD — as clear as it can get for someone on the outside anyway. These adults deserve a standing ovation for having the courage to open their lives to us and for flying in the face of the shame so often unjustly correlated with ADHD. I certainly offer an immense gratitude.

Penny

The names in the book have been changed to protect the privacy of the individuals who were so gracious about sharing a bit of their lives with the world. Many were open to me using their real names, but I decided their privacy was ultimately more important.

To know what it's like

The Vortex

"But it's only a DOLLAR!" a tiny person's voice commanded. "I can push it on the floor. Look! The wheels still turn. I don't need the remote. It rolls!"

"No," his mom answered. "I explained to you when we came into the store that I would buy you a book here but nothing else. You just bought toys with your allowance an hour ago. What you want now is broken." She remained very calm, addressing him in a matter-of-fact tone.

He bellowed a fierce groan into the air, and the books he'd chosen earlier hit the floor with force. "I don't want these books!"

There was no longer any restraint in his tone or volume. People nearby were pretending to look at merchandise about the shelves, but their gaze and attention couldn't help but join this family's escalating predicament.

"Son, it's time to leave," the mom said. Her calm demeanor was admirable. "I am happy to buy the books for you, or you can choose to leave without them. We need to get in line to pay now if you'd like to buy the books."

"I don't want those stupid books! I want a car!"

"That's your choice," she reminded him, voice still calm, unwavering. "Let's return the books to the shelf where you found them so we can go."

His brow was furrowed, but his eyes were wide and sinister. "NO! I'm not leaving! I'm not leaving unless you buy me that car!"

At this point, the boy's father snatched the books out of his hands and returned them to the shelf. He came back around the corner to the tight aisle where this little man had planted himself between the two cars he wanted. "We're leaving now," the father said sternly, and he headed straight for the exit.

His mom began to follow and found her load suddenly much heavier as the boy pulled backward on her coattail, screaming in defiance from deep within.

"I want the books! I want the books! I want the books!"

She was able to pull enough to get outside, but they were standing smack in front of the automatic doors, held open by their presence like a stage curtain for the entire store audience.

She continued to try to reason with him, explaining that his opportunity to have the books had passed, but he had already crossed the line and fallen headfirst into full-blown meltdown. There wasn't any stopping this barreling train now. They had to ride it to the end of the line.

She headed for the car and asked the boy to follow her. He wrapped his arms around the purse hanging from her shoulder and leaned in the opposite direction with every ounce of his weight. As he leaned back, their feet became entangled, and they succumbed to imbalance and gravity. It's a wonder they didn't topple to the pavement, but she managed to regain physical composure. No luck with emotional composure though — anger set in.

She had kept calm and remained rational up to this point. She knew his behavior was not within his control, that he was hyper-focused on those second-hand toy cars, and he just didn't possess the neurological skills to snap out of it and move on. But now he had almost caused physical harm to them both, a reality she wasn't going to accept. She grabbed his arm and physically escorted him to the car. His father and sister had been inside the car for several minutes now.

The boy and his mom stood behind the car as she tried to talk him down before they got in together. He was now punching her in the stomach with his tiny fists and repeating, "I want the books!" over and over and over. Tears were pouring down his little face.

"I know you want the books, Buddy," she said with great empathy. "I wanted you to have those books, too. But I can't buy those books for you when you were so ugly to Momma." She paused a moment to prevent her own tears. "I know you understand that."

She begged him to let her hold him and give him a big squeeze to help him calm down. They were way past that point though, and he repeatedly swatted down her outstretched arms.

His father emerged from the car to use force to end the madness. Mom asked him to let her handle it, reminding him that she could more easily remain calm.

"He's not going to hit you and scream at you like that. I'm not having it! We need to go," his father proclaimed, metaphorically putting his foot down.

He grabbed the boy's arms and lifted him into the car. The boy stretched his arms and legs out in all directions as far as he could to try to prevent it, but he was placed in the car. The force angered his mother.

She got in the front seat and sat silently.

The boy began to kick the back of his father's seat with great power, like a prizefighter hitting a punching bag, all the while crying and repeating, "I want the books. I want the books. I want the books." On the third iteration, he would scream it from way down in his throat at the highest pitch he could reach. It was as if his brain were a record or CD stuck in a scratch, repeating the same small section of recording again and again and again.

His sister sat next to him in a panic. She tried to offer him everything she owned in an effort to distract him.

The parents asked her not to interfere, not wanting to reward his behavior or allow her to.

The father demanded that the boy buckle so they could go.

The boy silently refused.

"You can choose to be safe or not, but I'm starting the car and going home," his father warned him.

His sister began to scream. "No, Daddy! Buckle! You have to be safe. Buckle!"

She reached across him to buckle his seatbelt, but the boy wiggled and swatted to prevent it. She began writhing and screaming and crying. She was slipping into a panic attack and about to melt, too.

"We don't have anywhere we need to be," Mom reminded her husband. "We just need to wait it out. He's saying the exact same loop over and over, and he's obviously not in control of his actions anymore." This was no longer a fit to get what he wanted. It hadn't been for a long while.

They sat for a minute or two longer, and the boy's behavior started to slowly key down. Mom offered him a snack, and he accepted. He was thinking of something other than the books, a clear sign his brain was releasing the fog. The boy buckled his belt as his father retrieved a snack from the trunk. Once they were all settled and ready to go, the mom grabbed her husband's hand and squeezed it. Tears streamed down both their faces.

Within minutes of pulling out of the parking lot, the boy was weeping and apologizing for his behavior. "I don't know why I act like that sometimes," he cried. "I'm so sorry! I didn't mean to hurt you, Momma."

* * *

Did this mom and dad handle this difficult situation effectively? Should the mom have tried threats of discipline, shame, or guilt to force the boy to pull himself together, follow instructions, and show his parents respect? Maybe, if she had told him she would take away his allowance, he would have complied? Or offered a punishment of no television for a week? What if she would have begun mimicking his behavior right there in the aisle of the store, to show him what he looked like? Would any of those tactics have provided better results — ended the boy's outburst sooner?

That's exactly what most parents would likely resort to when faced with this situation. On the surface, it looks like a discipline issue. But is it really? This book will explore which of the myriad of conventional parenting tactics are truly effective for kids with ADHD from the perspective of adults who were once kids very much like this boy, adults who understand on some level what it's like to be this boy. Adults who grew up with ADHD.

* * *

I would venture to guess that, if you're reading this book, you have likely experienced an episode similar to this boy's meltdown — maybe many. As excruciating as this scene is for the parents, try to imagine how traumatic it must be for the child. What does it feel like to literally not be in control of your words, thoughts, and actions?

What is it like to realize you've hurt your family when you truly didn't intend harm? What does it feel like to have your brain *hijacked*?

That story could belong to any family dealing with ADHD — add names and the players and scenery change, but the enormity of the emotional vortex remains largely similar.

This is actually *my* story though. I am the boy's momma, and the boy is my son, Ricochet. This happened to my family when stopping by at a Goodwill store one Saturday evening when my son was about eight years old. I purposefully say that it "happened to us" — no one could have foreseen it, or changed it, and no one was to blame. This episode was the first time I truly understood that sometimes my son had absolutely no physical control over himself — that his brain was sometimes hijacked. This epiphany came *two years* after his ADHD diagnosis. After two long years of reading everything I could find on ADHD, every day.

I would have given *anything* to know how to rescue my son in those moments. I knew to remain calm for the best possible outcome by then, but I didn't know how to help him calm down or prevent the episode altogether. It troubled me terribly to think of Ricochet's deep shame and the fact that I couldn't take that pain away, or even stop it from occurring again in the future. I desperately wanted to know what it's like to be a child with ADHD like Ricochet, so I would have the insight necessary to help my sweet boy.

Gaining Insight

Wouldn't it be great if parents *could* crawl inside the minds of our kids with ADHD? To know what the world is like from their unique vantage point? To feel the anguish that stems from emotions and behaviors sometimes out of your own control? To experience being punished for behavior you don't have the capability and skills to manage? To know what it's like to feel as though you're incapable of matching your peers' successes? To not be able to understand others beyond the literal definitions of the words they speak? To agonize over the sense that no one in the world understands what it's like to be you?

Come to think of it, that doesn't sound so great after all. It sounds wretched!

However, knowing what our kids with ADHD go through day-to-day — to experience it first-hand so we really, truly understand their struggle — would be a gift to these kids and to us, their parents.

While that's not scientifically possible, gaining perspective on what strategies are and are not helpful from adults who grew up with ADHD offers a great deal of awareness. It's a pearl of wisdom I've longed for over the last seven years and a gift I've worked hard to construct and now share with you.

It's the gift of insight and understanding so *critical* to the happiness and achievement of our kids and to the health and happiness of our entire families.

What ADHD Feels Like

No one can possibly understand what it feels like to grow up with and live with ADHD, unless they have ADHD themselves. I don't think a true understanding can be gained through first-hand descriptions either, but that's all we parents have to go by when we don't have ADHD.

In order to provide as much insight as possible, I participated in some online simulations of inattention, organization and time management issues, and writing struggles. I gathered descriptions and analogies from adults with ADHD as well.

Disability Simulations

The simulations, called *Through Your Child's Eyes* on Understood.org, are designed to help parents of kids with invisible disabilities understand their child's day-to-day experience. Every child's experience is unique, but *Through Your Child's Eyes* can offer valuable new insights into what it *feels* like to have learning and attention issues. I encourage you to participate in these online simulations yourself by visiting http://bit.ly/ThruChildsEyes.

I found the simulations wildly frustrating, especially the simulation for attention issues. In the attention issues simulator, the environmental noises are magnified so that it's very hard to focus on and hear the teacher's instructions for the activity. I personally was only able to complete 30 percent of the activity in the simulation because I wasn't able to filter out the teacher's voice from all the other sounds going on in the classroom, plus intrusive sounds from outdoors. I felt my frustration build to anger as the other students around me were preventing my success by talking. I was helpless to succeed. Once I reached the end of the activity, I felt down and defeated. It was a truly overwhelming emotional experience, and I didn't have the added pressure of knowing my teacher was going to be irritated that I didn't get my work finished or of getting a bad grade and disappointing my parents — the end result of the activity didn't count for me as it does for our kids in the classroom each and every day.

For the organization and time management issues simulator, I had to move the bucket to catch particular shapes. Sounds simple, and it seemed simple at first. Yet, each time I figured out how to catch the shapes, the rules changed and I had to very quickly formulate a new plan. That mimics how kids with organization and time management struggles feel every day.

I feared I was not going to be able to override my impulse to throw my computer at the wall while taking the writing issues simulator. I type pretty fast, and not being able to type what I was supposed to, despite actually hitting the right keys, was infuriating. That simulates what it feels like to know what you want to write but to not be able to get it out correctly. This is an issue my son knows all too well. I certainly wouldn't be a writer if I had dysgraphia as my son does. I would avoid any activities, schoolwork, and jobs that required much writing, too.

While I consider myself to be very knowledgeable about ADHD, learning disabilities, and my own son's issues in particular and in great detail, this was a very eye-opening exercise for me. I found all the simulators Understood.org offered very overwhelming. Each made my anxiety well up to an emotionally charged level. I was frustrated and angry during each simulation. I felt defeated and devastated by the end. It's disheartening to realize that our kids have these experiences and emotions every day, but that insight will make us better parents and advocates for our kids' special needs.

I also gathered some illuminating analogies of what it's like to have ADHD, as conveyed by a variety of adults living with ADHD. This provides a much broader insight than simply my experience, or your own, on a couple of online simulators.

How Kids and Adults with ADHD Describe What It's Like

In order to broaden the scope of insights of what it feels like to have ADHD, I gathered analogies and descriptions from kids and adults who have ADHD. Really dive in to these likenesses. Savor every word and visualize the experience described in your mind and heart. Let yourself be vulnerable and try to extrapolate the emotions offered in these depictions. Submerse yourself in the pictures you'll paint in your mind's eye to receive more than an explanation — to absorb the feelings and emotions of daily life with ADHD.

*"People that meet me find me intelligent, friendly, funny, attractive, kind, and relatively normal. I say this because these are the qualities that have made diagnosing ADHD so difficult. I can do many things and have some strengths in creativity and other areas. It is when I am tasked to do **detailed, mundane, repetitive** things that I come apart at the seams. Furthermore, loud noises, clutter, paying bills, and household chores can send me over the edge. I want to run and hide from the **barrage** of sensory over-stimulation. Every person has a unique experience with ADHD, so what may be true for one may not be true for others. I'd like to give you a little look at what my experience has been.*

"Imagine there is a room full of people, and you are told that these people have some information to give you in order to accomplish something important. You're also told that some of that information is critical and that you must retain it along with the name of each person. In addition, you're told that you must track the movements of each person as they walk about the room. As each person delivers their information, you try to store it in memory and track their movement as they walk away. As you're trying to memorize the information and track the person's movements, more people are approaching you with their information.

"As you're still trying to focus on the first people, the new information coming in begins to cause a low hum in your head. The hum gets progressively louder to the point where you cannot distinguish what people are saying. Suddenly, you realize that you are

probably missing some important information, and you try to break through the hum to collect it. Now you've lost track of the first person and begin to feel panic. You start looking for the first people in order to recollect their information, but you can't, because you're still collecting from the others. Now every bit of information that breaks through the hum carries the same weight. There is no way to distinguish what is most important. You try to start over, but you've already forgotten many of the first bits you've collected. It's a losing battle, and eventually you give up on that task and berate yourself for failing.

"Take this scenario and apply it to virtually everything you have to do to function in life. It's impossible.

"Now you want to prove to yourself and others that you are not an idiot, so you move on to the next task you think you can do. If that thing is in line with something that highly interests you, you may be able to hyperfocus and be successful. However, life is challenging even for someone who doesn't have ADHD, and that brings a whole new set of problems. Add to the mix the responsibilities we have to our friends and family and their expectations of you as a normal person, and you have the perfect picture of potential failure.

*"Once you complete the cycle a few hundred thousand times or more, you become defensive every time someone says, **'What's wrong with you?'** or 'I just told you that, don't you remember?' or **'You need to try harder'** or 'You only care about yourself' or **'You're just making excuses.'** Sadly, those are only some of the nice things people say.*

"Soon, people begin to dismiss you or call you names and even laugh at you. They try to force you to do what they themselves can do. They are struggling to manage their lives and yours, and they learn that you will step up your efforts if you feel bad enough.

"Soon, you begin to avoid interactions with people and even isolate yourself, just so you can feel a little break from the onslaught. However, this too is perceived as being selfish and uncaring. You may begin to defend and retaliate in order to protect any remaining self-worth. This causes severe mistrust and conflict. Meanwhile, depression has been creeping into the picture, and you are not aware of it until it has you in its claws. You begin to play the victim because you believe they must be right. The psychological impact of this is incredibly **damaging to self-esteem** and personal growth. The impact of this on careers and relationships is not hard to see.

"Now you vow to fight on and try harder because you know that, deep in your heart, you are a loving person who wants to contribute and share in the bounties of life that others seem to enjoy so easily. You so desperately want to please others and be accepted, but you live in a secret world of shame and self-loathing. You begin to believe that there really is something wrong with you and that you must be a bad person. You begin to step up your efforts to cover your tracks, so that you can show your loved ones you care. The problem is, you are being judged as a normal person and people are beginning to only see you for your failures, further compounding the ugly

feelings. Bring to the table life's confusion of careers, family responsibility, finances, and people's personal baggage, and you have a no-win situation."
—Rick

*"Living with ADHD is **like walking up a down escalator.** You can get there eventually, but the journey is exhausting."*
– Kathleen

*"ADHD is like a **never-ending** train wreck."*
— Gary

*"Every single night, almost without fail, dinner time rolls around and everyone is hungry and wondering what's for dinner, including me, the STAY AT HOME MOM!!! Really. It's like **the movie Groundhog Day**. I have to relearn or re-remember the stuff I'm supposed to do every day. It's funny but also really frustrating."*
— Joyce

"It's a million things running through your mind all at once and your mind can't stop or pause on any one. It just keeps going around and around with what you want to do, need to do, should do, haven't done, forgot yesterday, and so much more, until you are mentally exhausted and did nothing, because you couldn't figure out what one thing to do in the time you had.

"It's the equivalent of watching the rest of the world going by, and everyone seems to know a secret that I don't. [That secret] allows them to manage life

effectively, and I am just flailing my arms wildly,
trying not to drown *in the pool of life. I desperately*
want to know what everyone else knows."
—Teresa

With ADHD, "your thoughts are interrupted. What
*I love about ADHD is that often **everything is***
intriguing *and wonderful. New ideas and changes*
are not strange to me, they're exciting. But that
enthusiasm never leaves. It's not just about the bright
and shiny, it's about ideas, songs, creative [activities] I
like. It's as though I have several tabs on my Internet
browser that I visit interchangeably. Unless it's
something that I'm really into — then I hyperfocus
and I lose track of time, food, and responsibilities."
— Mary

> *"Quite often, it is rather like having a lined sheet*
> *of paper full of things that need to be done (or you*
> *want to do) that is slightly **'out of focus'** until you*
> *force your mind to pick one. Sometimes it feels like*
> *viewing a menu with all your favorite things listed,*
> *but you can only have one. Sometimes it is like*
> *watching a kaleidoscope that you have no real control*
> *over. Things just keep changing. Just when you <u>see</u>*
> *the thing you need, it moves out of view."*
> *— Dorothy*

*"To me, it's like when you have **too many tabs***
open *at once on the computer, and the computer*
slows down and often freezes because it's overloaded."
— Nicole"

*Having ADHD feels like always being **a bit out of step**. Like everyone knows the steps to a dance but you, so you're always trying to keep up and observe what you're doing that's not quite right. It's a sense of knowing you are different — sometimes in blatant ways, sometimes in subtle ways."*
— Terry Matlen, Author of Queen of Distraction

Gathering Deeper Insight

I started this project because I wanted to know what parenting strategies are beneficial for kids with ADHD, as well as those that are not, just like any parent of a child with ADHD. Since I didn't grow up with ADHD and don't have ADHD myself, I had to research, survey, and interview those who do. The only way to truly know what individuals with ADHD found beneficial or detrimental as they grew up was to ask those very individuals. So that's exactly where I began.

My online survey for teens and adults with ADHD (see Appendix A for the full survey text) was the initial vehicle to gather much of the information presented in these pages. I offered responders anonymity in order to get as many responses as possible. Yet, most chose to submit their names and contact information to help with my project in any way they could. As I dug into the survey responses, I quickly learned this willingness was not only an illustration of their acceptance of ADHD, but also of their own struggles growing up different and misunderstood. Their generosity is golden, and we owe them an abundance of gratitude. Their openness will make us better parents to kids with ADHD and change our kids' lives for the better.

In the end, I compiled ninety-five responses from individuals with ADHD ages fourteen to seventy-four. As expected, the responders were mostly female (78%), but that doesn't invalidate my data when the same threads are woven throughout the answers from both males and females. A whopping 68% of the responders were diagnosed after age twenty, a sign of how far popular understanding and medical science has come in recognizing and understanding ADHD in the last fifty to sixty years.

What I learned from these individuals with ADHD will improve your child's life and yours by extension. While every individual with ADHD is just that, an individual, the common themes I uncovered help build a wonderful parenting foundation for all kids with ADHD. Some of the approaches suggested are parenting tactics that all parents should use, not just parents of kids with ADHD and behavioral and developmental special needs. However, these approaches are more important, crucial really, when parenting kids with ADHD. Many of these suggestions are the hinge point between success and failure.

Gender of Survey Responders

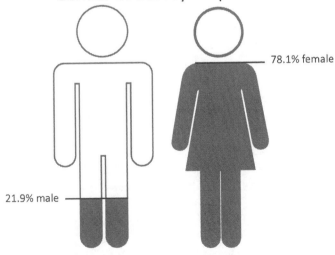

78.1% female

21.9% male

Current Age of Survey Responders

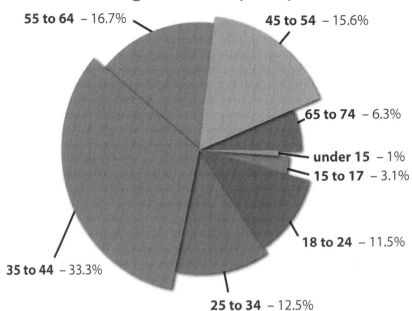

55 to 64 – 16.7%
45 to 54 – 15.6%
65 to 74 – 6.3%
under 15 – 1%
15 to 17 – 3.1%
18 to 24 – 11.5%
25 to 34 – 12.5%
35 to 44 – 33.3%

Age Responders Were When diagnosed with ADHD

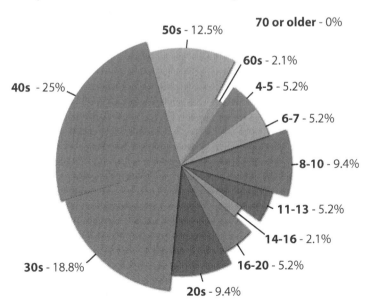

50s - 12.5%
70 or older - 0%
60s - 2.1%
4-5 - 5.2%
6-7 - 5.2%
8-10 - 9.4%
40s - 25%
11-13 - 5.2%
14-16 - 2.1%
16-20 - 5.2%
30s - 18.8%
20s - 9.4%

What is ADHD?

By Definition

If you're reading this book, you likely already know what ADHD is. Your child is inattentive, or impulsive and hyperactive, or all of the above, and in all facets of life. Your child has likely already been diagnosed, yet you're still struggling at school and at home. You've picked up this book in the hopes of finally getting a handle on this chaos in your family, this ADHD. You likely know what ADHD is, but let's define it anyway for those just starting on this special parenthood journey who may not have a clear understanding quite yet.

According to the National Institute of Mental Health, ADHD is defined as follows:

"Inattention, hyperactivity, and impulsivity are the key behaviors of ADHD. It is normal for all children to be inattentive, hyperactive, or impulsive sometimes, but for children with ADHD, these behaviors are more severe and occur more often. To be diagnosed with the disorder, a child must have symptoms for six or more months and to a degree that is greater than other children of the same age.

Children who have symptoms of inattention may:
- Be easily distracted, miss details, forget things, and frequently switch from one activity to another
- Have difficulty focusing on one thing
- Become bored with a task after only a few minutes, unless they are doing something enjoyable
- Have difficulty focusing attention on organizing and completing a task or learning something new
- Have trouble completing or turning in homework assignments, often losing things (e.g., pencils, toys, assignments) needed to complete tasks or activities
- Do not seem to listen when spoken to
- Daydream, become easily confused, and move slowly

- Have difficulty processing information as quickly and accurately as others
- Struggle to follow instructions.

Children who have symptoms of hyperactivity may:
- Fidget and squirm in their seats
- Talk nonstop
- Dash around, touching or playing with anything and everything in sight
- Have trouble sitting still during dinner, school, and story time
- Be constantly in motion
- Have difficulty doing quiet tasks or activities

Children who have symptoms of impulsivity may:
- Be very impatient
- Blurt out inappropriate comments, show their emotions without restraint, and act without regard for consequences
- Have difficulty waiting for things they want or waiting their turns in games
- Often interrupt conversations or others' activities."[i]

All or some of the symptoms listed above are part of what led to your child's diagnosis of ADHD. They interfere with life a great deal, especially school and family time. As parents, we want to help our children overcome these hurdles as much as possible. Just how to do that successfully can be a mystery to most families.

People refer to ADHD as many different things — a condition, a disorder, a disease, a disability. Which is correct? In my mind, calling it any of those other than disease would be pretty accurate. However, I'd be wrong. Merriam-Webster defines disease as "an illness that affects a person, animal, or plant; **a condition that prevents the body or mind from working normally;** a problem that a person, group, organization, or society has and cannot stop." ADHD fits that definition to a T.

So, how should we explain ADHD to others? I like to call it a neurological and/or physiological condition that affects development and behavior. I feel that it's extremely important to impart the knowledge that ADHD is really a physical abnormality, even though it's an invisible one (except maybe on an MRI scan of the brain). So many people think it's just bad behavior, or bad character, and that doesn't help our kids one bit. By referring to ADHD as a "neurodevelopmental disorder" (where it is now categorized in *The Diagnostic and Statistical Manual of Mental Disorders – 5th edition*), you are sharing that it's a neurological difference and a developmental delay all in one term, which gives others a truer depiction of the real struggles of ADHD, rather than just the idea that it's an inability (or unwillingness) to manage behavior.

All the Other Elements of ADHD

ADHD is much, much more than the brief diagnostic list outlined above. This definition is just a starting point — a means to establish a diagnosis and a treatment direction. What I'm here to add is the honest, down-in-the-trenches, living-it-every-day insight to raising a successful and happy kid who happens to have ADHD. In the chapters ahead, we will dig into the experience and wisdom only teens and adults who grew up with ADHD can offer in order to craft a very clear picture of what will help your child with ADHD triumph.

First, however, let's start with all the other facets of ADHD not mentioned in the diagnostic criteria and often not shared with families upon diagnosis. (There can be many coexisting conditions, too, like anxiety, depression, learning disabilities, autism, and more. I will not be covering those here, but you should be aware of the potential for co-existing conditions and keep an eye out for their symptoms.)

Sensory Issues

The SPD Foundation estimates that between 40 and 60 percent of children with ADHD or SPD will have symptoms of both disorders.[ii]

Sensory Processing Disorder (SPD), also sometimes referred to as Sensory Integration Disorder, is when the brain's signals in reaction to sensory stimuli cause an inappropriate response. An individual with SPD finds it hard to process and interpret sensory input and react accordingly. For instance, if they have SPD, your child might overreact to loud sounds or certain tastes or smells, or underreact to coarse tactile input.

Children with disabilities have markedly more sensory processing issues than children without disabilities.[iii]

In Dunn and Bennett's 2002 study of sensory processing patterns of children with ADHD, they found that kids with ADHD displayed sensory behaviors more frequently than kids without disabilities. The children with ADHD had significantly lower scores on more than half of the sensory items in the auditory, touch, multisensory, emotional/social responses, and behavioral outcomes categories of the *Sensory Profile*.[iv]

This demonstrates a significant correlation between ADHD and SPD.

Many studies have shown substantial sensory issues for children with ADHD in the following categories of senses:

- Kids with ADHD have more difficulty processing tactile input. They can be hypersensitive, seemingly overreacting to touch or pain, or they can be hyposensitive, seeming not to feel touch.
- Kids with combined-type ADHD (inattentive and hyperactive/impulsive) have more issues with balance and coordination.
- Kids with ADHD have more difficulty with auditory processing than kids without developmental disabilities. It's not that they can't hear or can't hear well, it's that their brain doesn't process what they hear accurately.
- Kids with ADHD are more sensitive to smells.[v]

Sensory impairment can lead to inappropriate responses to sensory stimuli.[vi] Think about Ricochet in the Goodwill store: sensory impairment could have certainly contributed to his eventual meltdown. The store was visually chaotic, loud, and filled with fluorescent light, which can agitate kids with SPD.

SPD affects more than just reactions to sensory input though. Sensory issues can be distracting and overwhelming, impacting cognitive processing and academic success, too. If your child with ADHD is having outbursts at school, consider the environment and any sensory triggers that might be causing a negative reaction — harsh lights, lots of noise, loud sounds, an overwhelming number of visuals, and a feeling of being too crowded can contribute to behavioral issues and outbursts.

Always consider sensory processing issues as part of the overall picture of ADHD.

Poor Executive Functioning

Many refer to executive functioning as the CEO of our brains. Executive functions are the mental skills that help the brain successfully act on an idea. They govern just about everything we do in our daily lives. More often than not, these skills are poorly developed in kids with ADHD.

Executive Functioning involves planning, organization, memory, time management, and flexible thinking. Not only do these skills affect the obvious like planning and organization, but they also affect self-awareness, emotional regulation, and flexibility.

Poor executive functioning is pervasive — it can disturb all aspects of a person's life, from cleaning up your room to school and homework, even daily hygiene and how one reacts to frustration.

Many portions of executive functioning can be improved through teaching and scaffolding, and there are strategies to work around these weaknesses, as well. We will discuss this more in *Chapter 4: What Does Work*.

Self-Esteem

Success may come easy for some, but I can promise you, it does not come easy for those with ADHD. They start off with the deck stacked against them when they enter school, an institution designed for those with a skill set opposite that of kids with ADHD. At school, kids are asked to sit still and focus for long periods of time. They are asked to do as instructed without question and without deviation. They are usually told there's just one way to do things, and creativity is often not welcomed.

When kids can't meet all those expectations no matter how hard they try or how much they want to, they begin to think there's something wrong with *them*. They see their peers do things they simply can't, no matter how hard they try, and it fosters a sense of being stupid, bad, or broken. Due to those underlying messages, good self-esteem — one's sense of self-worth — is doubly hard to achieve when you're a kid with ADHD.

Don't lose hope! I didn't say healthy self-esteem is *impossible* with ADHD, I simply said it's much more *difficult.* Parents can help a great deal, and we will dig into that deeper in *Chapter 4: What Does Work.*

Shame

A child's identity is shaped by the things they hear about themselves from others. Many are taught to keep their lips buttoned tight about ADHD,

> SHAME:
> noun \'shām\
> a painful emotion caused by consciousness of guilt, shortcoming, or impropriety

as if it's a closely-held, dark family secret. Keeping ADHD confidential implies that it is something to hide, to be ashamed of. For kids and adults alike, this further perpetuates the negative messages so common for those with ADHD — "You're lazy," "You're always late," "You don't try hard enough," "You're not meeting your potential," etc... — and the feeling that there is something *wrong* with them, that they are defective. In the words of Rick, who so clearly described his perspective of what it's like to have ADHD for us in Chapter 1, "You begin to believe that there really is something wrong with you and that you must be a bad person."

A culture of shame in childhood can create an adult who cannot accept the positive, or even find joy, because the message of defect becomes ingrained. The shaming messages become that individual's inner voice and can consume them. While shaming may cause conformity through fear, its detriment is powerful, potentially leading to long-term psychological damage and conditions such as anxiety, depression, and self-medication with alcohol and/or drugs.

The path to success and happiness for an individual with ADHD does not allow shame. Accept that ADHD is a neurological condition, not a lack of moral character, and be open about your child's ADHD. The only way others can help your child on their journey is to know your child's strengths and weaknesses and understand how their brain works (as much as possible, anyway). And the only way that can happen is by being open and honest about ADHD.

Inflexibility

Kids with ADHD are often described as rigid or inflexible. It's not that they're stubborn or selfish, it's that they simply don't have the skills to rationalize, adapt, see more than one way in any given situation, and manage frustration appropriately. Inflexibility is often the trigger of many a public meltdown (like my Goodwill shopping experience with Ricochet described in Chapter 1 of this book, and shared in my previous book, *Boy Without Instructions*).

Concrete thinking — seeing things in a very literal way, without any interpretation or generalization — is often a part of what appears to be inflexibility, too. Concrete thinkers may not perceive analogies and relationships. Many kids with ADHD live by definition. When something is open to translation, such as an analogy or figure of speech, they take it at face value, very literally. If it's not intended literally, their misunderstanding and insistence on the way they see things can seem rigid and/or lead to an outburst.

Once, when Ricochet was maybe seven or eight years old, I was deep in the muck of my own frustration with his inflexibility when I mumbled under my breath, "You'll be the death of me." He began to cry, "No, Momma! I don't want to kill you. I *love* you." As much as I tried to explain a figure of speech to him that afternoon, he simply couldn't understand it. He felt certain that I said he was going to be the one to end my life.

This kind of literal thinking can create problems with schoolwork and even in the most mundane daily interactions with others, especially peers. Here's another example of how concrete thinking can interfere in a child's day-to-day interactions:

> The instructions on the sixth grade math worksheet read, "Solve each problem. Show your work." Ricochet, my very literal, concrete-thinking son, completes the worksheet on time and gets 80% of the problems correct. Yet, his teachers keep asking him to "do more" and "show your work." Ricochet argues that he did show his work and points to the portions of the problem-solving process he had to write down on some of the problems. He was able to do part of the work in his head, but he doesn't see how to show that and doesn't realize that the work he does in his head is part of the "Show your work" portion of the instructions. He doesn't understand why his teachers keep telling him he isn't finished, and his teachers

think he's being willful and defiant. Everyone involved ends up frustrated, and Ricochet gets points deducted for "refusing to show his work."

Inflexibility, for whatever reason, can be very difficult for parents to deal with. If your child gets "stuck" in these ways, I urge you to read *The Explosive Child: A New Approach for Understanding and Parenting Easily Frustrated, "Chronically Inflexible" Children*, by Dr. Ross Greene. His approach to understanding and working with inflexible kids is powerful and very effective.

Intensity

Intensity in kids with ADHD stems from five constants: (1) hypersensitivity, (2) perceived disapproval, (3) low frustration tolerance, (4) poor emotional regulation, and (5) sensory sensitivities.

Hypersensitivity causes an abnormal, exaggerated response. This can present in someone with ADHD through a high level of sensitivity to physical and/or emotional stimuli. If you feel your child often reacts to things in a manner way outside what the situation dictates would be an age-appropriate response, they very well could be hypersensitive.

Individuals with ADHD often perceive disapproval where it doesn't necessarily exist or respond more intensely to criticism and rejection. Dr. William W. Dodson, of the Dodson ADHD Center, identifies this phenomenon, called rejection-sensitive dysphoria, as part of ADHD. "It is the constant vulnerability to being 'wounded' by anyone at any moment that continues to throw them into a tailspin without warning, and then disrupt their lives for days with obsessive worry about 'What did I do to make them hate me so much?' It does not even have to be real rejection or criticism (although that is common enough in the lives of people with unrecognized and untreated ADHD). Perceived criticism and withdrawal of love and respect are just as devastating as the real thing," Dodson explains on his center's website. Rejection-sensitive dysphoria can lead to defensiveness and outbursts of anger.

Kids, and many adults, with ADHD typically have little frustration tolerance. They quickly get over-emotional when frustrated, lacking the skills to work through disappointment and aggravation appropriately. Frustration often escalates to anger, and an outburst far out of scale from what the situation truly warrants can unfold.

One has to be aware of their own emotions before they can regulate them, yet many kids with ADHD have a tough time labeling and expressing how they are feeling, especially in any detail. And emotional regulation requires not only that awareness but also the skills to affect your own mood and emotions. Without this self-regulation, kids with ADHD often express a significant emotional intensity.

Sensory sensitivities can also yield emotional intensity. A situation could be too stimulating and overwhelming for the child, or the child could be hypersensitive and every little sensory stimuli feels overwhelming and crushing.

Most kids with ADHD are very intense. If you find yourself often saying, "It's not the end of the world" or "Act your age" to your child with ADHD, they likely struggle with emotional intensity.

Seeming Lack of Motivation

Individuals with ADHD are often told to "try harder," especially in school and work environments. Yet, what looks like they "just don't care" is due to their atypical neurology — it's *not* a character flaw. People, **it's not a character flaw.**

Most people have an importance-based nervous system, meaning they can focus on what is important, whether it's of interest to them or not, simply because they are told it's important. Individuals with ADHD have what Dr. Dodson has dubbed an "interest-based nervous system." The "interest-based nervous system works well, using its own set of rules," says Dodson, rules based on stimulation through interest, novelty, challenge, and urgency.[vii]

When someone with ADHD doesn't complete an important task just for the sheer fact that it's important, it isn't defiance or a lack of caring on their part, nor is it a character flaw or a moral issue. It's simply the difference in how their brain creates motivation.

Crushing ADHD Myths

I cannot emphasize enough the importance of understanding ADHD and the complexities it creates in your own child. The adults who took my survey relayed this same message time and again — the symptoms aren't a moral or character flaw, and they aren't a sign of laziness or stupidity, they are part of ADHD. Let's look at some specific ADHD myths and the facts that crush them.

Myths	Facts
ADHD is not real.	ADHD is a neurodevelopmental disorder — a difference in the way the brain grows and develops. Through brain imaging, researchers have discovered that the brain matures the same, but about three years behind.[viii] Brain imaging also shows a distinct difference in brain matter and activity in those with ADHD.
Bad parenting causes ADHD.	A parent can dole out all the punishment in the world, and it will not make a lasting improvement on ADHD symptoms. No amount of discipline will control impulses the brain cannot control. More discipline isn't the answer, but rather a specific type of discipline that works with your child's differences.
Children outgrow ADHD.	There is no cure for ADHD.[ix] While some children with ADHD can manage pretty well as adults, ADHD symptoms still affect most throughout their lives.[x]
Giving a child ADHD medication is getting them "high," just as if you'd given them speed.	ADHD medications counteract the symptoms that affect day-to-day functioning. They balance the neurotransmitters in the brain to better mimic "normalcy." One cannot get "high" with the doses prescribed for ADHD and under doctor supervision.[xi]

Myths	Facts
Only kids who are hyper have ADHD.	There are three types of ADHD: inattentive, hyperactive, and a combination of the two. One can struggle with inattention but not be hyperactive and still have ADHD. Some experts say that those with inattentive ADHD have hyperactivity, too, but in their minds, not their physical activity level.
ADHD can be cured by special diets or supplements.	There is no cure for ADHD.[xii] Many studies have been done on special diets and other natural treatments, but the results so far show little to no efficacy across the board.
People with ADHD just need to "try harder."	ADHD is a neurological condition, and motivation is generated neurologically. People with ADHD generate motivation through interest, not importance. These individuals do try hard — harder than most realize or give them credit for.

Now that we have our facts straight and ADHD characteristics thoroughly defined, we can move on to the experiences of those who have grown up with ADHD — positive and negative — and learn from them.

What Doesn't Work

The Hippocratic Oath, "First do no harm," comes from early Greek medical texts, requiring physicians to uphold certain ethical standards. Due to its origin, it is correlated with the health care industry in our society. Why do we limit it to only physicians? Shouldn't it be a human standard? I challenge parents and teachers to apply the Hippocratic Oath to their own personal parenting standards as well. In *everything*, first, do no harm. Including when parenting kids with ADHD.

In parenting challenging kids, exhaustion, frustration, and struggles for power can cloud our judgment of "harm" or push us further and further away from seeing it clearly. Studies show that harmful parenting tactics are much more detrimental than effective, and the adults with ADHD who took my survey support that, too.

I asked the survey responders to rate different types of motivation based on how effective each was for them as a child. Following are the types of motivation they rated.

- My own desire to do well
- Praise from teachers
- Punishment from teachers
- Being shamed by teachers
- Praise from parents/family
- Punishment from parents/family
- Being shamed by parents/family
- Being made to feel guilty by elders
- Being made fun of by peers
- Being ostracized by peers
- ADHD medication
- Help from therapist and/or coach
- Teacher believing in me
- Parents believing in me
- Coach believing in me
- Support of my church
- Support of other community member

Their choices on the rating scale were:
- This was a huge motivator! Motivated me every time!
- This helped to motivate me.
- This didn't make a difference one way or the other — didn't motivate me or demotivate me.

- This was a real downer — often made me less motivated rather than more.

Once compiled and graphed, the results speak for themselves.

Sources of Motivation as a Child with ADHD

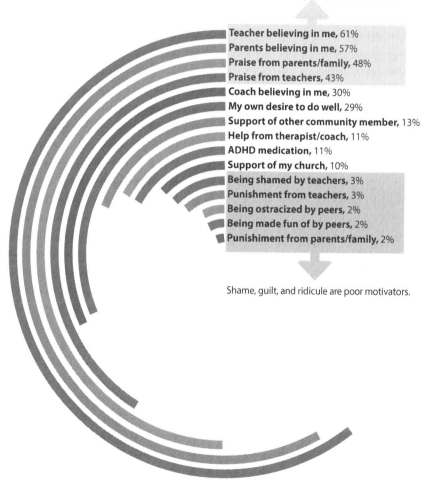

Praise and positivity are the best motivators.

Teacher believing in me, 61%
Parents believing in me, 57%
Praise from parents/family, 48%
Praise from teachers, 43%
Coach believing in me, 30%
My own desire to do well, 29%
Support of other community member, 13%
Help from therapist/coach, 11%
ADHD medication, 11%
Support of my church, 10%
Being shamed by teachers, 3%
Punishment from teachers, 3%
Being ostracized by peers, 2%
Being made fun of by peers, 2%
Punishiment from parents/family, 2%

Shame, guilt, and ridicule are poor motivators.

Shame, guilt, and ridicule don't motivate kids with ADHD, and, as we will discuss in detail now, are just plain ole bad parenting. We will look at *What Does Work* in depth in *Chapter 4.*

Emotional Manipulation

Often, parents resort to tactics like shame and guilt to punish a child or make their point in a memorable way. It's intended to make an impact, illicit obedience, and illustrate who is boss in the relationship. The problem is that this type of parenting, called emotional manipulation or psychological discipline, does more damage than good — it creates a toxic relationship and often leads to psychological harm for the child.

In her article, "Toxic Adults Affect Kids Too: Know the Signs and How to Explore a Little Deeper," psychologist Karen Young says, "Toxic relationships are ones in which someone's own negative behavior can cause emotional damage or contaminate the way a child sees himself or herself. They can lead to anxiety, depression, physical illnesses, and feelings of isolation. Children can end up blaming themselves and feeling guilt or shame. Even if there is something about our kids that needs a little bit of a nudge in a different direction, any behavior that makes them feel less than or ashamed just won't do it. In fact, it will do damage."[xiii]

We all have been guilty of emotional manipulation of our kids at one point or another. Yes, I said "we." In researching for this book, I realized that I am sometimes guilty of this parenting strategy, too, at least the guilt tactic. I point out to my children how their actions make me feel far too often.

> "Don't you know Momma worries about you when I don't know where you are?"

> "How do you think it makes me feel when you treat me like that?"

For some, emotional manipulation has been passed down through the generations —that's the way their father raised them and their grandmother raised their father. While that explains how they came to parent in this way, it certainly doesn't make it right or effective. Most probably do it inadvertently. We don't mean to "manipulate" our children. We (meaning I) just want them to know we have feelings, too, and that they hurt us sometimes. Whether intentional or not, emotional manipulation is not a sound or effective parenting approach, especially for kids with ADHD.

The themes of guilt, shame, and ridicule came up again and again in the ADHD survey responses of adults. I imagine that's because frustrated parents finding that traditional parenting tactics don't work for their kids with ADHD often escalate the punishment to try to force compliance.

> "If Tom won't stop talking back when I take away his iPad, I bet he will when I take away all his electronics."

Let's take a deeper look at what constitutes emotional manipulation in parenting and how it does more harm than good, especially in kids with poor and fragile self-esteem, like kids with ADHD.

Shaming

As parents, it's our job to provide safe harbor for our children. Shaming them, even to make a point, doesn't provide that sense of safety it is our duty to provide our children, the sense of safety they deserve. None of us is perfect though, and we all lose our patience and/or our grip on sanity at one time or another. A parental slip-up here and there is human, but a consistent style of parenting that relies on shame does more harm than good.

> "Taking money out of my wallet without asking is **stealing**. You're a **thief**!"

> "You're a liar! You should be ashamed of yourself for doing that."

If you are on social media, you've probably seen posts by parents intending to shame their kids into doing what they are asked and walking the proverbial line. There was the dad in North Carolina who posted a YouTube video of himself shooting his daughter's laptop with a gun because she claimed on her Facebook page that she is a "slave" and should get paid for doing chores. In June 2015, a thirteen-year-old girl in Tacoma took her own life after her father cut off all her hair as punishment, filmed it, and posted it on YouTube. Hundreds of parents have forced their kids to hold up signs in public places, advertising their "crimes" for all the world to judge. Dozens of parents publically sold concert tickets they purchased for their kids as a punishment for offending behavior. What message do these types of public punishment really send? Not the messages parents think.

Shame actually makes a child feel incapable and defeated, the very feelings common to kids with ADHD that we are trying to improve. Ironically, parents use shame to push kids to a perceived higher level, when, in actuality, it only breaks them down.

Parents aren't the only authority figures guilty of shaming as a form of discipline and control. Some teachers are guilty of it, too, such as when Ms. Gulch holds up Johnny's essay with a big red D scrawled across the page and parades around the classroom, announcing that it's an example of what *not* to do.

Except for a few, almost all the responders to my ADHD survey said shame from parents and teachers made them feel *less* motivated, not more. I think it's probably a valid assumption to conclude that the few who found shaming motivational have high anxiety.

Shaming a child is a way of demanding respect for parents, but it has the opposite effect — it is instead disrespectful and breaks down trust. If you don't respect your child, how will they learn to respect you? Shaming also teaches kids they cannot trust you not to humiliate them. Again, parents should be a safe harbor for kids, and they can't be without a fundamental trust.

Instead of condemning the behavior, as it is meant to do, shaming ends up being received as a personal attack.

Shame and humiliation make kids feel worthless, incapable, stupid, and bad. It can also lead to depression, anxiety, and increased stress.[viv] No one wants that for their kids.

Studies show using shame to teach and enforce right from wrong and establish authority can lead to aggressive behavior, too.[xv] That's the opposite of the perceived outcome of this type of discipline.

Shame is created from judgment through the values of *others*. "You should be ashamed of yourself because you know I don't approve of this behavior." Children are a reflection of their parents in most cultures. Often parents enlist public judgment to show that their kids have deviated from their personal values or societal expectations. It's almost a move of self-preservation for the parents, but the cost to the child is much more detrimental than it is to you when others simply think you might be a "bad" parent.

Guilting

Guilt teaches kids to think about the emotions of others and form empathy, a needed lesson. However, frequent and consistent guilt is psychologically damaging.

Like shame, guilt is a form of emotional manipulation or psychological discipline. In contrast to shame, guilt is derived from our own values and judgment of *ourselves*, rather than societal expectations. "I should be ashamed of myself because I don't approve of my behavior."

When a child is forced to feel guilty for something they did or caused, parents are essentially passing the burden of the stressful situation on to their child. The

Being Shamed by Parent/Family
(Rate the following sources of motivation when you were a child with ADHD)

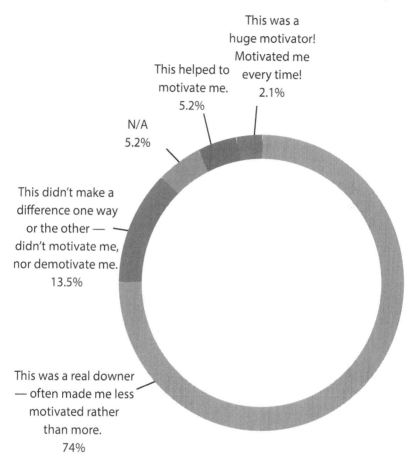

This was a huge motivator! Motivated me every time!
2.1%

This helped to motivate me.
5.2%

N/A
5.2%

This didn't make a difference one way or the other — didn't motivate me, nor demotivate me.
13.5%

This was a real downer — often made me less motivated rather than more.
74%

Being Shamed by Teachers

(Rate the following sources of motivation when you were a child with ADHD)

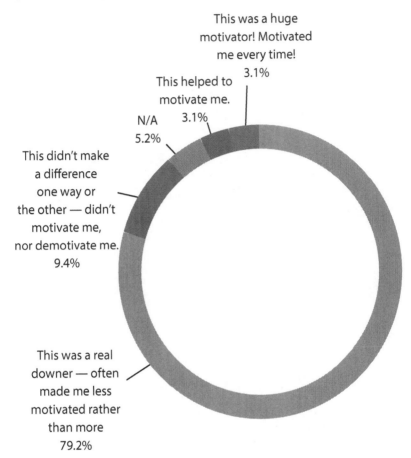

This was a huge motivator! Motivated me every time!
3.1%

This helped to motivate me.
3.1%

N/A
5.2%

This didn't make a difference one way or the other — didn't motivate me, nor demotivate me.
9.4%

This was a real downer — often made me less motivated rather than more
79.2%

child causes the parent stress, so the parent passes that pain to the child by making them feel guilty about it.

> Julie's mom loses her temper when Julie finally arrives home an hour late.
>
> "Don't you know I worry half to death when I don't know where you are?" she scolds.
>
> Julie apologizes and heads straight to her bedroom, her gaze firmly planted on the floor, proverbial tail between her legs.
>
> She feels awful for making her mom worry and apologizes again and again for several days.
>
> She keeps thinking she's stupid and unlovable because she did something to upset her mom.

Making our kids feel guilty as a way of controlling their behavior is not suitable parenting. Guilt-inducing parenting leads to more distress and anger in children, even the following day.[xvi]

Greater still, one study found that pathological guilt in childhood actually changes areas of the brain and increases the risk of depression in adulthood for that individual.[xvii]

Our kids' brains are already different enough; let's not add to their struggles with dangerous parenting maneuvers!

Guilt can be compounded into internal shame as well. The child might think, "I'm such a terrible son. I constantly make my mom worry. If I were a good child, I wouldn't cause my mom stress." Shame and guilt go hand in hand.

Your reflex might be to punish the one who caused you that stress, but that's not healthy for anyone. When a situation has you stressed, take a break instead of passing the burden on to your child. Remind yourself that this is *your* stress and yours alone to deal with.

We parents all make mistakes at one time or another with our kids. We don't need to worry about a guilt-trip here or there. However, consistent guilt-inducing tactics can do lasting psychological harm to your child.

Using guilt as an answer to ADHD behaviors is especially dangerous. Kids with ADHD are already more prone to low self-esteem, endure a higher level of stress, and often have additional psychological issues such as anxiety and depression. Studies of the effects of guilt as a parenting tactic prove that we are only increasing the odds of these types of mental health issues for kids with ADHD.

My ADHD survey shows that guilt is a largely ineffective motivator for kids with ADHD anyway.

* * *

The most effective tactic for parenting and teaching kids with ADHD is a positive reinforcement approach. We will dive into that in more detail in *Chapter 4: What Does Work*.

Being Made to Feel Guilty by Elders

(Rate the following sources of motivation when you were a child with ADHD)

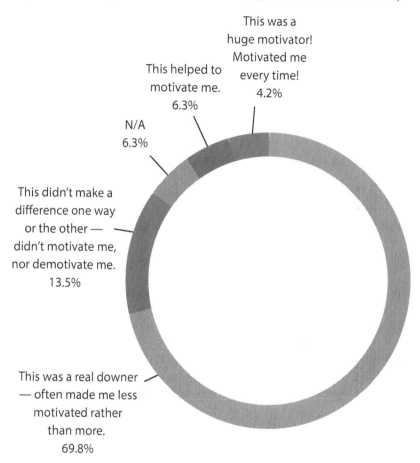

This was a
huge motivator!
Motivated me
every time!
4.2%

This helped to
motivate me.
6.3%

N/A
6.3%

This didn't make a
difference one way
or the other —
didn't motivate me,
nor demotivate me.
13.5%

This was a real downer
— often made me less
motivated rather
than more.
69.8%

What Doesn't Matter as Much as Parents Think

There are certain parenting assumptions we all learn through our culture, family, experiences, and environment. For example, most of us are taught that grades, academic performance, and extracurricular participation are crucial to success in life. I grew up thinking grades were super-important because I was punished when I had anything lower than a B on a report card. Good grades get you into college; a college degree gets you a career; a career brings financial stability; and financial stability ensures success and happiness. That's the "American Way" at least, and I was taught no different.

My experiences over the last seven years — my son's school years — paint a different picture — one in which grades aren't necessarily a measure of knowledge or a predictor of future success, and just getting to school and staying the entire day without a meltdown or trauma can be reason enough to celebrate. (You can read all about our school experiences in *Boy Without Instructions* too.)

Grades

When Ricochet began school in 2007, the proverbial s@#t hit the fan in an instant. That is a seriously appropriate analogy, trust me. His kindergarten teacher called me on the second day of school and asked me to come in and meet with her. *Really?! It's only the second day of school! Give the kids a chance to settle*, I thought. She felt his behavior those two days was attributable to far more than the newness of attending school. He couldn't stay in one place and keep to himself. He couldn't sit still and pay attention long enough to get through story time. He didn't understand personal space, evidenced by the purple and yellow splotch on her chin that afternoon from when Ricochet had popped up like a jack-in-the-box and collided with his teacher.

As we trudged through day after day, week after week of kindergarten, my focus wasn't on skills and learning, but on just getting through one day without a scathing note coming home from his teacher, or a tongue-lashing through the car window at pick-up. *Who cares if he knows how to write his name, as long as he didn't naively and inadvertently piss someone off?* That's where I lived his entire kindergarten year — slogging through each and every day and pining for summer break.

The following year, a new school and new teacher didn't help Ricochet's ability to perform as expected in the classroom. In desperation, I spoke to his pediatrician, and she sent us for a behavioral and developmental evaluation. That fall, he was diagnosed with ADHD. Finally, the school nightmare made sense. There was a reason Ricochet couldn't meet expectations — his brain works differently.

I thought that knowledge would provide the clarity needed to facilitate success at school. I thought the hard part was over. I had a lot to learn!

Two years later, just a short time into third grade, his teacher recognized his handwriting disability, and he was included in special education for more support for his learning disability. *Finally*, I thought, ***this*** *is what he needed;* ***now*** *he can succeed.*

Nope. I was still naïve when it came to learning difficulties and ADHD. My first whiff of the smelling salts came in the form of a tiny black letter D on Ricochet's first report card that school year. A D in writing. It was my first D. It was far more crushing than if I had earned that D myself. In my mind, it signified my failure as this special boy's momma.

When I became more rational about it the following day, I realized it wasn't me who had failed Ricochet, it was "the system." The school didn't accommodate his needs adequately enough, so *they* are the ones who failed him. It was that moment of logic that sparked the light bulb — no matter what a child with a disability does, or how much support their parents give them, sometimes the very best they can do is a D, especially in a world not designed for special learners. I had to throw those grades-mean-everything ideals I grew up with out the window and accept that grades aren't an accurate measure of success for some kids. I realized that grades and extracurriculars are not that important for all students. They just can't be. There is a better measure of academic success for kids with ADHD and/or learning disabilities.

The majority of adults who completed my survey agree grades shouldn't be the highest priority for parents raising kids with ADHD, or academic performance in general. Just 20% of responders answered that academic performance overall is very, very important, with only 11% feeling grades were very, very important. In contrast, a whopping 80% of responders said that grades, as well as academic performance overall, matter but that some or many other things are more important.

Academic Performance Overall

(Based on your personal childhood experience, rate each of the following on importance for parents to focus on when raising a child with ADHD.)

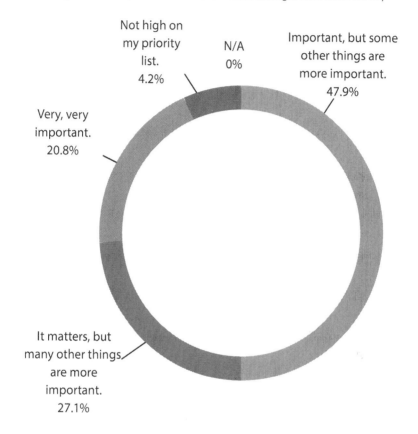

Not high on my priority list.
4.2%

N/A
0%

Important, but some other things are more important.
47.9%

Very, very important.
20.8%

It matters, but many other things are more important.
27.1%

Grades

(Based on your personal childhood experience, rate each of the following on importance for parents to focus on when raising a child with ADHD.)

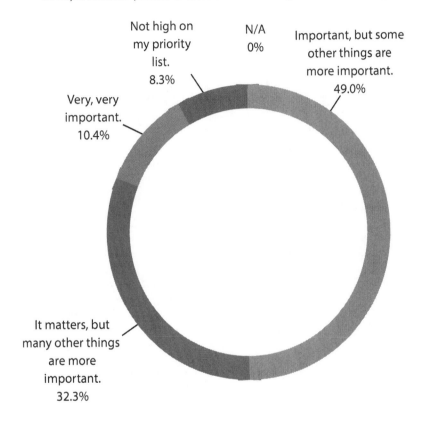

Not high on my priority list.
8.3%

N/A
0%

Important, but some other things are more important.
49.0%

Very, very important.
10.4%

It matters, but many other things are more important.
32.3%

As I discuss in my previous book, *What to Expect When Parenting Children with ADHD*, you have to craft a different yardstick of expectations to measure success for kids with ADHD— for your own sanity and for their self-esteem and confidence.

Popularity

Likeability or the number of friends one has is also often used as a measure of success in our culture. Parents work diligently to set up play dates and other social opportunities to foster friendships for their kids. While a feeling of social connectedness is an important component for happiness, a large number of friends is not.[xviii]

The survey results show that adults with ADHD concur that the number of friends one has is not a very important focus for children with ADHD — the number of friends doesn't influence happiness and achievement. Only one responder said that having many friends is very, very important. Yet 39% said having many friends is important, but some things are more important, and 43% said having lots of friends matters, but many other things are more important to emphasize in parenting kids with ADHD.

The tables were turned, however, when asked how important a child having close friends is to the focus of parents raising kids with ADHD. 46% of responders said that close friends are very, very important, and 41% said close friends are important, but some things are more important to focus on. That means 87% of survey responders feel that the quality of relationships and social connectedness are more important than simply the number of friends one has.

Having Lots of Friends

(Based on your personal childhood experience, rate each of the following
on importance for parents to focus on when raising a child with ADHD.)

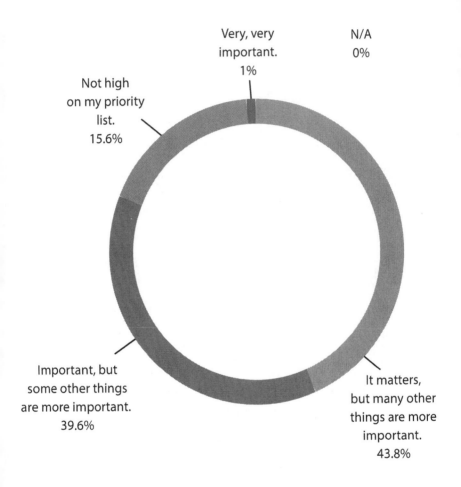

Very, very important. 1%

N/A 0%

Not high on my priority list. 15.6%

Important, but some other things are more important. 39.6%

It matters, but many other things are more important. 43.8%

Having Close Friends

(Based on your personal childhood experience, rate each of the following on importance for parents to focus on when raising a child with ADHD.)

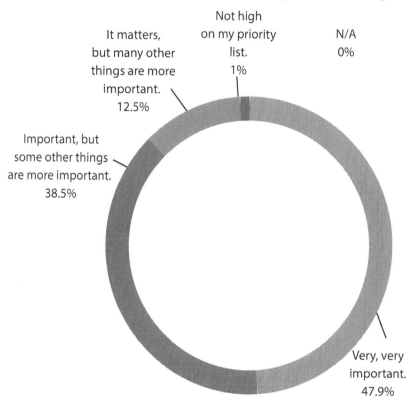

It matters, but many other things are more important.
12.5%

Not high on my priority list.
1%

N/A
0%

Important, but some other things are more important.
38.5%

Very, very important.
47.9%

A number of studies back up these results and further describe the role friendships play in happiness and self-esteem. It is the closeness and frequency of contact in friendships that positively affect one's happiness.[xix] In a 2006 study published in the *Journal of Happiness*, Melıkşah Demır and Lesley A. Weitekamp found that "friendship quality predicted happiness above and beyond the influence of personality and number of friends... Additional analyses revealed that the companionship and self-validation features of friendship quality were predictive of happiness..."[xx]

Kids with ADHD struggle with social relationships. It's most important for parents to facilitate and nurture quality relationships for their children — don't worry about them having a great number of friends.

Sports

Studies show that playing sports has a positive effect on child development. Kids learn cooperation, teamwork, confidence, competence, and leadership from participating in sports. Those skills result in better grades, stronger self-esteem, deeper connections with others, greater family attachment, and more restraint when faced with the opportunity to participate in risky behavior.[xxi]

It's important to note, however, that this research is based on neurotypical child development. When you add in the challenges of ADHD symptoms, the outcomes change to varying degrees.

Let's be clear. I'm not saying that kids with ADHD shouldn't play sports or can't be successful at sports.

Playing Sports

(Based on your personal childhood experience, rate each of the following on importance for parents to focus on when raising a child with ADHD.)

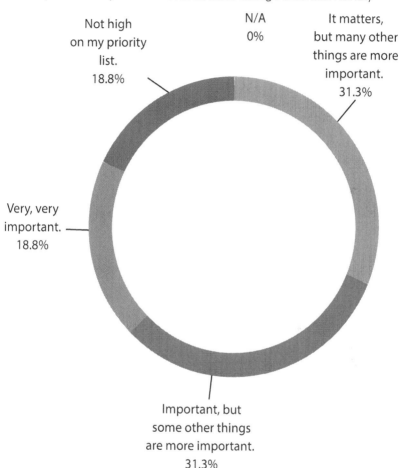

Not high on my priority list.
18.8%

N/A
0%

It matters, but many other things are more important.
31.3%

Very, very important.
18.8%

Important, but some other things are more important.
31.3%

There are many professional athletes with ADHD — Michael Phelps, Cammi Granato, Terry Bradshaw, Pete Rose, Shane Victorino, and Andres Torres, to name a few. Many find that the hyperfocus common with ADHD can be an asset during intense training and the challenge of the game.

The adults I surveyed had pretty mixed opinions about how important they feel participating in sports is for kids with ADHD. While an equal percentage are each on the outer rims of importance, thinking it's very, very important or not a high priority at all (18% each), 65% think some or many other things are more important.

That makes it tough to know where to draw the line when it comes to emphasizing sports participation for our kids with ADHD. It's really a decision to be made by weighing your child's unique constellation of strengths and weaknesses. Ricochet had too much hyperactivity for baseball, too slow a processing speed for soccer, and too much anxiety for swimming. He did find long jump and shot put in track and field enjoyable for a while but just wasn't motivated at ten years old to choose it over chilling out at home in the shady, cool air-conditioning. I plan to offer him the opportunity to do track and field again when he's a teen.

My conclusion, taking into account all the published research on youth sports and child development, as well as the results of my survey, is that sports are definitely a benefit if they are right for *your* child. If they are not a good fit, there's no benefit to be gained, only stress, anxiety, and worsening self-confidence.

What Does Work

Now we've come to the treasure within these pages — what people who grew up with ADHD feel is most crucial to raising happy and successful individuals with ADHD. While they may fly in the face of traditional parenting strategies, the insights revealed here are largely common sense. If you can escape traditional parenting paradigms and customs, you will be able to raise a happy and successful kid who happens to have ADHD.

Will it happen immediately or all at once? No way! There's a significant learning curve to parenting a child with ADHD successfully. It's a marathon, not a sprint.

You are building the foundation, setting the stage for success, by implementing with your own child the experience and wisdom of those who have taken this particular journey already.

Kids with ADHD are motivated by a few simple things: praise from family and teachers, parents and teachers believing in them, and a positive approach.

Larry, an eighteen to twenty-four-year-old adult diagnosed between the ages of ten and thirteen, shares how important praise has been to motivate him at school: "I was always the worst at completing homework; however, the teachers that took the time to talk to me and figure out a way to motivate me (treat, praise, motivation, compassion) [caused] a significant rise in how much more important it was for me to complete a certain task. This remains true to this day."

Beyond motivation, there was one overarching question on my mind to ask adults who grew up with ADHD: "What advice would you offer parents raising kids with ADHD? Something you wish your parents or teachers did? Something you wish you did for yourself? Etc...."

This question was wide open for a multitude of responses, but obvious themes emerged right away as I began to study their answers. Pictures are worth a thousand words, so let's start there in order to see these obvious patterns and themes.

What is Most Important

(Based on your personal childhood experience, rate the importance of these factors for parents to focus on when raising a child with ADHD.)

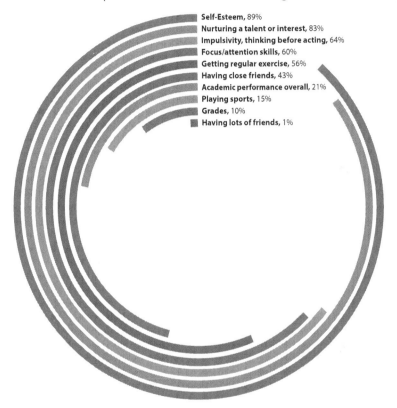

Self-Esteem, 89%
Nurturing a talent or interest, 83%
Impulsivity, thinking before acting, 64%
Focus/attention skills, 60%
Getting regular exercise, 56%
Having close friends, 43%
Academic performance overall, 21%
Playing sports, 15%
Grades, 10%
Having lots of friends, 1%

1

Self-Esteem

(Based on your personal childhood experience, rate each of the following on importance for parents to focus on when raising a child with ADHD.)

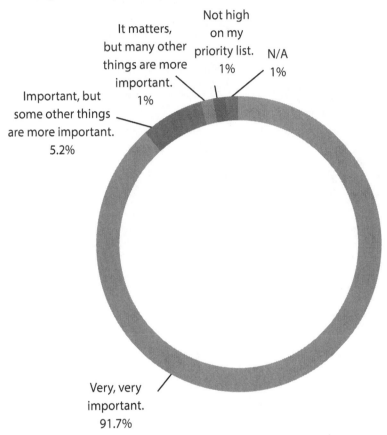

It matters, but many other things are more important.
1%

Not high on my priority list.
1%

N/A
1%

Important, but some other things are more important.
5.2%

Very, very important.
91.7%

2
Nurturing a Talent or Interest
(Based on your personal childhood experience, rate each of the following on importance for parents to focus on when raising a child with ADHD.)

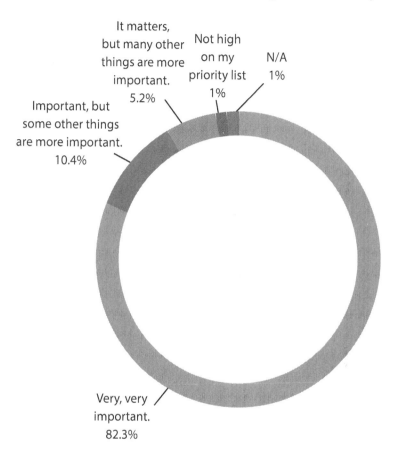

It matters, but many other things are more important.
5.2%

Not high on my priority list
1%

N/A
1%

Important, but some other things are more important.
10.4%

Very, very important.
82.3%

3
Focus/Attention Skills
(Based on your personal childhood experience, rate each of the following
on importance for parents to focus on when raising a child with ADHD.)

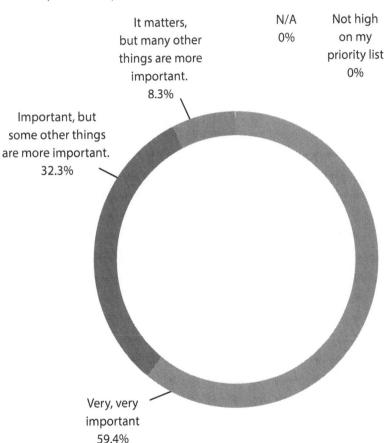

It matters,
but many other
things are more
important.
8.3%

N/A
0%

Not high
on my
priority list
0%

Important, but
some other things
are more important.
32.3%

Very, very
important
59.4%

Impulsivity and Thinking Before Acting

(Based on your personal childhood experience, rate each of the following on importance for parents to focus on when raising a child with ADHD.)

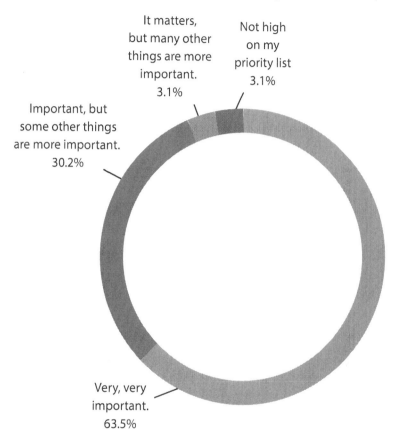

It matters, but many other things are more important. 3.1%

Not high on my priority list 3.1%

Important, but some other things are more important. 30.2%

Very, very important. 63.5%

Take note! The survey responders placed importance on focusing on self-esteem and nurturing talents and interests *above* focusing on improving inattention and impulsivity, the hallmark weaknesses of individuals with ADHD. I found that most interesting. It supports what experts like Dr. Edward Hallowell advise — take a positive approach and focus more on strengths than on weaknesses. It also reflects the responders' input on effective sources of motivation as kids with ADHD:

- praise from parents, family, and teachers;
- parents and teachers believing in them (supporting them);
- and a positive approach overall.

Offering your child successes is more important than helping them overcome the symptoms of ADHD itself. I'm going to say that again so it really sinks in:

Offering your child successes is more important than helping them overcome the symptoms of ADHD itself.

This is a huge revelation — by nature, parents want to fix what's wrong above all else. The survey responders, adults who grew up with ADHD and who know what it's like to be a child with ADHD, tell us that should not be our first priority — helping them feel successful and confident should be.

All the data on the chart boils down to one thing:

Discover,
listen to, and
accept your
child's unique
truth.

Here are twelve parenting ADHD truths that all lead you to discover your child's individual truth — what is true for *them* — through Understanding, Positive Parenting, and Building Lagging Skills:

1.	Knowledge is power.	**UNDER-STANDING**
2.	Interest fuels focus.	
3.	Validation offers relief.	
4.	Love conquers all.	**POSITIVE PARENTING**
5.	Calm is crucial.	
6.	Positivity and praise inspire self-esteem.	
7.	Support adds strength.	
8.	Appropriate expectations bring relief.	
9.	Every child has strengths and talents.	
10.	Meet kids where they are.	
11.	Skills aren't always inherent, but can be taught.	**BUILDING SKILLS**
12.	Accommodations provide fairness, not destroy it.	

Let's look at each parenting ADHD truth in detail so you can implement these truths in the way you parent your child with ADHD.

Knowledge Is Power

Learn All You Can About ADHD and Offer Treatment

"Learn as much as you can about ADHD and put systems in place as early as possible," recommends Keith, whose ADHD was diagnosed in grade school. I strongly concur. You can only do your best for your child if you truly understand every facet of their strengths and weaknesses and seek answers to their own particular and unique why's. Read all you can about ADHD. Talk to others who have ADHD or who are also raising a child with ADHD. Go to workshops, classes, and support groups. Dig deeper to consider co-existing conditions like anxiety, depression, or learning disabilities.

"Research all you can, reading books, Googling, and talking to professionals. If you are having trouble coping with [your] child, seek help and don't stop trying. Stand up and be heard. Reach out to all the [resources] available and join the ADHD parenting groups, either in person or online," suggests Nicole, a woman diagnosed with ADHD in her twenties. "Hearing about other people with similar lives made me feel a little less isolated. I never liked the thought of medication for my child, but it made such a difference in my own life, I could not hold that back from maybe giving my child a chance to feel like days can be easier. I don't think medication is a cure, but with other strategies and lots of support from friends and family, I have learned to cope."

"Educate yourself. Understand that every solution to ADHD is a personalized solution — there is no one-size-fits-all answer," advises Anne, a woman diagnosed in her forties. "Understand the age lag in your child. Understand the importance of exercise for ADHD."

"Seek professional advice for your child if you are not sure what to do," advises Mary, who also wasn't diagnosed with ADHD until her forties.

"Information can be retrieved within seconds today," offers Jill. "Your child needs strategies, life skills, critical thinking skills, and a great sense of self. Do whatever you can to help them achieve that. Learning disabilities and ADHD are not always easily recognizable."

Be open to different treatments, including medication. If you're nervous about a particular treatment, read all you can about it so you can make an informed decision. The common social sentiment about ADHD medication is not factual. It's not like giving your child "speed" — it brings their brain up to a more normal level of stimulation by increasing the level of neurotransmitters needed for focus and attention — it does not increase stimulation above the norm, which is what "speed" does. Your child is not going to get "high" from an appropriate dose of medication for their ADHD and under a doctor's supervision.

The dangers of stimulant medication are not as severe as many believe either. According to the Child Mind Institute, a non-profit and clinical mental health practice in New York, "Stimulant medications are controlled substances, which means they have a potential for abuse, though they are not considered addictive at the doses prescribed for ADHD."

"Get appropriate treatment for your child," offers Mark. "This may or may not include stimulant medication. However, any medication should be just one part of an overall plan, which should also include talk therapy, tutoring, and school accommodations."

Learn about medication dosing and side effects. "Make sure they are on the right type of medication so that they don't have the zombie feeling," offers Frannie. If a child is experiencing the "zombie effect," that means their dose is too high, or their current medication isn't right for them. ADHD medication takes a lot of tweaking, so prepare yourself for that and work with your child's doctor closely to ensure the benefits far outweigh the side effects.

Am I trying to convince you to give your child medication? No, not at all. I am simply encouraging you to learn the facts and consider them before making your decision about ADHD medications. That's what many of the adults with ADHD recommend as well. Several of them talk about how they wish they'd had treatment sooner, and they wonder if they would have struggled less if that had happened.

"Keep reminding yourself that your child's odd, frustrating behavior is due to factors outside their control," advises Jake, who was recently diagnosed in his forties. "Understand that procrastination is a huge part of ADHD," says Naomi, who was also recently diagnosed, in her fifties.

Many adults who grew up with ADHD will be the first to tell you that they felt "stupid," "lazy," "bad," or "broken" as a child. Too many of them still do. These were the messages they received throughout childhood when people around them didn't understand ADHD or didn't even know they had a neurological difference.

Has your child ever told you they are "dumb," "lazy," "bad," or "broken?" I know my son has, many times, and he is none of those things. He didn't hear these accusations from our family and likely only heard them blatantly spoken a few times, but these are the messages he, and other kids with ADHD, internalize when they are misunderstood and undervalued.

"I struggled the past twenty-eight years of my life thinking I was stupid, different from everybody else, depressed, and ashamed," shared Leslie, "until this year when I accepted the diagnosis and learned about it. Reflecting back, my life would be much different had I been treated in high school. I wonder where I could have gone with my life."

Before we knew Ricochet has ADHD, learning disabilities, and autism, my sister married her husband, Mike. Three years later, Ricochet was diagnosed with ADHD. At that point, Mike began to talk about how he has ADHD, too, diagnosed as a child but never treated successfully. In the seven years since, Mike has talked to me many times about his kinship with Ricochet and how much he understands and relates to him.

Recently, standing in my kitchen, Mike said to me, "I never thought my life could be good. You know? I have a loving relationship, a wife, a daughter, and a job I enjoy. I always thought my life would be dysfunctional. I thought all the self-medicating and the constant carousel of job failures was the best my life could be." He paused to sustain his composure. "It was crap. For so many years, I never thought anything better was possible."

That conversation has haunted me every day since. Mike has a very supportive and understanding mom (whom I *adore*) but was still misunderstood by most people in his life— throughout his childhood and even still as an adult. He received those same unspoken messages of being "bad" and "broken." He had a life of struggle and failures over several decades so consistent that he thought happiness and success were not in the cards for him — *ever*.

Growing up misunderstood can have lasting effects and severe consequences on one's entire life. Late blooming is common for people with ADHD, but they should not have to feel like happiness is unattainable for forty years until they finally find their success. Since Mike sees a lot of himself in Ricochet, I worry that Ricochet, too, may feel he's doomed to a life of failure. I can't let that happen.

This has been a fear for me ever since Ricochet's diagnosis. Will he always struggle? Will he be able to find success? Happiness? It's my own fear, and I have to own it, but I knew it was a very valid fear nonetheless. Now, hearing all these adults validate that common parental fear has fueled my interest in crafting and sharing this book even more. It certainly solidifies the need for such.

Get the facts about ADHD and work to understand your child on a deeper level. (My previous book, *What to Expect When Parenting Kids with ADHD*, offers a step-by-step guide for to get to know your child with ADHD on a deeper level.) Knowledge leads to understanding, and our kids need that so much — from their parents and everyone else in their lives.

Interest Fuels Focus

Keep It Interesting

As I touched on earlier, the ADHD brain is motivated by interest and urgency. Most people have an importance-based nervous system, meaning they can focus on what is important, whether it's of interest to them or not, simply because it's important. Individuals with ADHD have an "interest-based nervous system." The "interest-based nervous system works well, using its own set of rules," says Dr. Dodson, "rules based on stimulation through interest, novelty, challenge, and urgency."[xxii]

Did you know that "stimulating" and "attention-grabbing" are synonyms for "interesting?" That, in and of itself, illustrates why things of personal interest are more motivating to a child who struggles with stimulation and attention, i.e., ADHD.

Use the characteristics of the interest-based brain to fuel focus in your child. Tailor the activity to be as appealing to your child as possible. Use their personal interests to make a task fun. For example, if they prefer technology, allow them to create a slideshow or video for their project on the solar system. If they have to research and write an essay on an animal, let them choose the animal they are most interested in for their subject.

"Repetition and constant interaction kept my interest [in school]," said Stephanie, not diagnosed with ADHD until her forties. "My best memory was of a college professor whose class I had to take to help pass a math course. I hate math. I was absolutely terrible at it. I loved this class though because he was funny and always engaging. I never had a chance to drift off or lose focus."

Tune in to your child's learning style as well, and use that to further retain their interest. Most kids with ADHD are visual, tactile, or auditory learners. Incorporate those senses aligned with their individual learning style into the task or project as much as possible, too.

"Hands on activities were the best for me," explains Maggie. "[Parents and teachers should] talk about topics such as history and science. Play games to learn and keep it interesting."

"I think the best teachers in college were the ones that loved what they were doing and made it fun," Joanie added. "They used videos, reading, and props because, in general, people learn in different ways."

Not sure what interests your child? Start by simply asking them and listening to their answers. Not just hearing but *listening*. Don't brush off anything for being trivial, frivolous, or not leading to great things. Take note of what types of activities or subjects they gravitate toward. Offer opportunities in lots of different areas. Nurture their curiosity and imagination to reveal interests and talents, too.

Validation Offers Relief

In my opinion, the single most helpful strategy for parents of kids with ADHD is validating your child's thoughts and feelings by showing interest and empathy. Sometimes, their emotional intensity is fueled by talk of "overreacting," "acting like a baby," or "stretching the truth." Kids are people, too. Their feelings matter, even if they react in a manner out of scale for the situation and/ or their age. Minimizing or dismissing their thoughts and feelings makes them feel like their ideas and/or problems don't matter — like *they* don't matter. Validating their thoughts and feelings, in turn, makes them feel understood and loved — isn't that what we all crave in life?

Jeffery Bernstein, PhD, author of *10 Days to a Less Defiant Child*, says, "understanding your child is just as important, if not more important, than loving them." It's that powerful. "Contrary to what many frustrated parents may think, particularly during those stressful times of conflicts," writes Bernstein, "validating feelings is not condoning bad choices or giving in to defiant behavior. Validating your child conveys deep empathy."[xxiii]

In her 1993 book *Cognitive Behavioral Treatment of Borderline Personality Disorder*, Marsha Linehan, PhD, writes, "[Validation] communicates that [their] responses make sense and are understandable within [their] current life context or situation." This is true for ADHD, too. It means, while our kids' responses may seem out of scale for the situation or not age-appropriate, validating their feelings acknowledges that their emotions are understandable within *their* viewpoint, through the lens of ADHD. You're acknowledging that their feelings are real and true to *them*.

Let's consider an example of validating your child's feelings/emotions:

> Ricochet hangs out a lot with his cousin, Creative H. She is just a year younger than him, and they have many similar interests. Since I work at home, Creative H often comes over to hang out with us on days when there's no school. On this particular day, the two were getting along better than I think I've ever witnessed. They giggled and laughed all day long.
>
> At about four o'clock, I noticed that the laughing had stopped and the tone of Ricochet's voice had become a little stern. By the time I was able to head in there to see what was going on, Ricochet flew past me down the hall and threw himself onto his bed. He wrapped himself tight in a super-hot blanket, with just his furrowed scowl peeking out.

"Hey Buddy," I said compassionately. "Tell me what's going on."

"She kept fighting with me about taking one of my chairs. She wouldn't stop asking over and over, even though I told her it was up to you," he answered.

"Wow. <u>I bet that was frustrating for you, huh</u>?"

He nodded.

"We have two of those chairs, and you can only use one at a time. What if we let her borrow one?" I proposed.

"That fine." There was an awkward pause, and I could see he had more to say.

"You can tell me everything, Buddy. It's ok."

"She called me 'insane'," he yelled.

"Oh, sweetie. <u>That hurt your feelings, didn't it</u>?"

He nodded again.

"I know she didn't mean it. We all say things we don't mean sometimes when we're angry."

That little bit of validation and acknowledging how he felt (underlined portions of the example passage) turned a situation that would have been a two or more hour sulking, and maybe a meltdown, into thirty minutes of recovering from the hurt. In addition, had I not shown understanding of his feelings, he might never have told me the full story so I would know the root of his pain.

There are many ways to validate a child's feelings. Other useful validating phrases include:

"I know it's hard to wait..."

"That must have hurt..."

"It's hard when you don't do as well as you wanted to..."

"It feels bad to lose..."

"We all get angry when..."

"I can see you are feeling..."

"That can be really annoying..."

"I feel the same way when..."

"I bet you are sad because..."

"I know what you mean..."

"How can I help you?"

Besides making your child feel understood, you are teaching emotional regulation strategies by talking through their feelings. Emotional validation fosters appropriate emotional development and regulation, skills kids with ADHD certainly need help with.

Another way to validate our kids' thoughts and feelings is to give them a voice in treatment decisions. "The best thing my parents did for me as a child with ADHD was to allow me to make decisions about therapy and medication," wrote Ella. "They were very supportive of my voice when creating my 504 Plan and IEP, too."

It's not just up to parents to validate their kids' thoughts and feelings. Teachers can make an important impact in this area, as well. "The best thing a teacher ever did for me was make me feel important when it came to participation and my ideas and projects," shares Carson, whose ADHD was diagnosed very early at age four or five. Acknowledging a student's struggles can be validating also, when done in a positive manner.

Jill illustrated the impact of validation from teachers by sharing this story: "When I got something wrong on a test, my amazing teacher said to me, 'Take it home. Find the answer. Write it on the test for me.' I said, 'But I'm not showing you that I was able to study it and answer it on the test.' 'Are you finding the right answer?' she asked. 'Will you know what the right answer is when you enter it on the test?' 'Yes.' She responded, 'Then you showed me that you went home and learned what the right answer was. What more do I need to see?' I had never felt so relieved and understood in my whole life. This teacher inspired me to go into the field of education. I'm so thankful that I was in her class. I will never forget her."

Melissa sums it up: The best thing my parents did for me was "let me be myself." There is no greater validation than that, is there?

Love Conquers All

Unconditional Love is a Powerful Force

Love is certainly a powerful human influencer. Don't worry, I'm not going to pretend that love alone can solve anything, much less "cure" ADHD. However, love and support go a long way for a struggling, misunderstood child. And unconditional love — loving a child no matter what — really can change the course of a life.

Love shows acceptance. To love your child unconditionally requires that you accept their ADHD and all the weaknesses accompanying it. It doesn't mean that you like the fact that your child has ADHD. It doesn't mean you don't grieve from time to time. It just means that you accept that it's part of your family's lives and you don't fight its existence.

Science proves the power of love, too. Affection can help the brain and heart and feed the soul. Scientists have begun to study and understand the chemistry and biology of love. Dr. Kathleen C. Light of the University of North Carolina at Chapel Hill is studying the science behind our body's reactions to love. She found that a hormone called oxytocin makes us feel good when on the receiving end of loving, warm contact by increasing dopamine (that neurotransmitter that is deficient in individuals with ADHD; the one that ADHD medication increases). Hmmm. It seems love may be able to help those with ADHD more than we realize.

In a study by Bradley, Caldwell, and Rock published in the August, 1988 journal, *Child Development*, the researchers concluded that children who grow up in a nurturing environment do better in school, in the areas of both achievement and behavior.[xxiv]

When asked what the best/most helpful thing their parents did for them when they were children was, many of the survey responders recalled that their parent(s) loved them and they knew it. "I always knew [my mom] loved and respected me," said Colleen, despite the fact that she wasn't diagnosed with ADHD until her fifties.

"They always showed and told me that I was loved," said Nicole.

That unconditional love had a deep impact on those who were fortunate enough to receive it. (Unfortunately, many said they were not). "My aunt's unconditional love kept me positive about the horrible things I was going through," described Marlow, "because I knew that, in spite of my mistakes, I would always be accepted at home. So if I wasn't accepted at school, it didn't matter, because my family had accepted me."

"Unconditional love from my parents was a constant. It always gave me a positive outlook on life," shared Bob.

"For me," offered Dorothy, a woman enjoying retirement, "it was knowing that even if no one else in the entire world understood and accepted me as I was, my parents and siblings did. Home was the safest place to be." That security was powerful for Dorothy, and it will be powerful for your child with ADHD also.

The survey responders suggested the same when asked what advice they'd give parents raising kids with ADHD today. "Let your child know that you love them just as they are," recommended Lynn.

Mary advised, "Let them know *often* that you love them."

"Be kind," warns Samantha, who says her parents and teachers made her feel like a "problem child," since her ADHD wasn't diagnosed until her forties.

Calm is Crucial

Approach with Patience and Calm

The origin of the well-known proverbial phrase, "Patience is a virtue," is somewhat debated, although most attribute it to the poem, "The Vision of Piers Plowman," circa 1370. Obviously, humanity has acknowledged the advantage of a patient approach for centuries. Even the adults with ADHD who completed the survey agree that one of the best things a parent can do for a child with ADHD is to remain calm — at least five of them offered that this was the best thing their own parents did for them when they were a child.

When parents take a patient approach, they model appropriate behaviors — like tolerance and calm — for their children. Remaining calm also facilitates a clearer thought process when problem solving or during a crisis, skills important for everyone.

Remaining calm in the face of adversity is a learned skill. Knowledge about ADHD, inflexibility, behavior issues, and delayed development common with ADHD was my best tool in acquiring this skill for my own parenting. When my son was diagnosed, I read everything I could get my hands on about ADHD and/or sensory issues.

The more I read, the clearer my son's strengths and weaknesses became. The more we worked with experts in behavior therapy and occupational therapy, the more I understood about the causes and functions of his different behaviors. Once I understood the perceived functions these different behaviors served for him, the calmer I could remain in the face of those behaviors. I no longer saw them as willful, lazy, unmotivated, or disrespectful. I recognized that they were part of his different neurology, part of ADHD.

Calm in the face of adversity takes time and work, but is a true gift. The stress of parenting a child with ADHD is heavy enough, without adding constant discord and yelling. Kids with ADHD are very perceptive, too — the calmer you are, the calmer they are likely to be, and vice versa. Remaining peaceful and composed is a benefit to you both.

"Speak with the kind voice you use with someone you love, not the harsh voice you use with someone you detest," requests Kate, a woman diagnosed with ADHD recently, in her forties.

Simply making a concerted effort to always remain calm with your child with ADHD will cause a dramatic shift in your family dynamic and your relationship with your child. Seeking calm in the face of ADHD has provided positive differences I now see in myself, our family, and, most importantly, in Ricochet. It has truly shifted our family dynamic in a very beneficial way.

Before Ricochet's diagnosis seven years ago, he probably heard "Why can't you just…" multiple times each and every day (if he even heard what I said at all). He experienced someone raising their voice to him or using a stern tone at least once a day as well, multiple times most days. His undesirable behaviors seemed like nothing more than willful little boy defiance to us — it felt like he was not complying with parental requests just to get a rise. Ricochet's dad and I punished, we yelled, we mucked around in a deep sea of frustration that was rapidly becoming quicksand. Home life felt awful for all of us. It was always loud and tense and uncomfortable. We didn't yet know there was another way, a more appropriate way to parent this child. We didn't yet understand him.

Once Ricochet was diagnosed, I quickly submersed myself in all things ADHD. I read every book I could. I spent countless hours on the Internet researching. I stalked online forums to hear real-life parenting experiences as they related to ADHD. I wanted to know how to help my son, and I wanted to know right away.

It didn't take long for me to realize we were punishing him and yelling in instances that were not within his control at that time. I immediately made a conscious effort to not get riled up about ADHD behaviors. Easier said than done, but I was determined. In my fear of punishing Ricochet for behaviors he couldn't control, I swung too far in the opposite direction and began using ADHD as an excuse for everything. He began to feel like it didn't matter what he did because he could simply blame it on ADHD and all would be forgiven. That, too, was no way to parent this kid.

Then, about two years after his diagnosis, I read the book *The Explosive Child: A New Approach for Understanding and Parenting Easily Frustrated, Chronically Inflexible Children*, by Dr. Ross Greene. Reading *The Explosive Child* is, hands down, one of the best things I have done to date for Ricochet, and for our family. It opens a perspective on the process of frustration in these children that so perfectly explains the nuances of my child (and children with ADHD in general).

Now I had the knowledge to stop yelling at my son and work *with* him instead to resolve negative behaviors. Here are the steps to achieve more calm in the face of ADHD behaviors:

1. **Recognize that what looks like willful disobedience may not be.** The first step is to truly understand your child with ADHD and why they do the things they do, especially those things that look and feel like willful disobedience. I'm not saying that a child with ADHD doesn't have moments of willful disobedience like any other child; I am saying they are no more frequent than with a neurotypical child, despite seeming so. Most children with ADHD have very little frustration tolerance (we will talk more about the skill of frustration tolerance later in this chapter),

and many are also quite inflexible (discussed in *Chapter 2*).

2. **Guide them through frustration.** How many times has your child asked for something and then completely melted down when they didn't get it? When they are two or three years old, you expect that. When they are eight or nine years old, you think they should know better. At twelve, you think this sort of meltdown is ridiculous. You try to impose your will and put your foot down, and they spiral out of control. You think it's all because they didn't get their way. But it's not. That's right, they're not throwing a fit to strong-arm you into giving them what they want — it's not even a "fit" in that sense at all. They melt down because they don't have the skills to see that there's more than one option, and they don't have the skills to handle the frustration they feel when the one and only thing they know to be true in that moment isn't.

    You must not engage but remain detached during a meltdown. You do that by remembering that your child's behavior, as much as it may seem so sometimes, is not a personal attack on you. By not taking it personally, you have a much better chance of staying calm.

3. **Work together and teach your child with ADHD lagging skills in these moments.** If your child is frustrated because their playdate is cancelled, talk through the situation with them. Show empathy for how they are feeling

to validate their emotions. Talk about when you could reschedule it and what they might do when they get the opportunity to finally play with that child. Talk about what you might do with the original time instead, now that it's free. This not only teaches them to think through options, but it distracts both of you from being emotional about the situation. View everything as a problem to be solved and take the opportunity to teach problem-solving skills.

4. **Lastly, remember who really has control of the situation — you, the parent — even when it feels like your child is trying to control you.** Don't relinquish control to your child or to an undesirable situation. There are plenty of ways to regain control and authority besides raising your voice or laying down a mandate. In fact, engaging by raising your voice or threatening punishment if they don't act right will prolong the outburst, but remaining calm and detached will actually shorten it.

Start your journey to calm parenting by digging deep to really, truly understand the triggers and functions of your child's unwanted behaviors. Implement some simple calming techniques when you feel yourself getting frustrated or angry, too:

- Remind yourself that your child is acting like a child because they *are* a child.
- Put yourself in their shoes.
- Give yourself a time out.
- Take a walk around the block.

- Turn on some music.
- Hum a tune.
- Start singing a silly song.
- Close your eyes and take relaxing belly breaths, in through your nose, out through your mouth.
- Speak to your child in a whisper.
- Use positive self-talk: "I'm doing the best I can…"
- Go to bed early.
- Clean something.
- Physically shake out the tension in your own body.
- Have a moment of gratitude.

I can tell you from experience, once you are able to remain calm when frustrated with your child, you will be a much more effective parent. Do I stay calm all the time? Of course not, but I've come a long way, and our entire family feels better for it, especially my son.

Breathe in… Breathe out… Again! You can do this.

Positivity & Praise Inspire Self-Esteem

Of everything I learned from the adults who completed my survey, this was their number one recommendation for parents: focus on your child's self-esteem.

Optimism and joy feel so much better than fear and helplessness. Positivity and negativity are polarizing. Like oil and water, they don't mix. Positive people attract other positive people to them, and negative people attract other negative people to them — both are magnetic in that sense.

Several responders reminded parents to be aware of being too critical. Mark said, "Stop the constant criticizing! Kids need to feel they are okay. Find things to praise."

"The best thing you can do for your child is stay positive," Eva added. Positivity and optimism can change a life. In the case of ADHD, positivity steers you to focus on strengths more than weaknesses. That's exactly what kids need to override those negative messages they so often receive at school and from others who don't understand their differences. Evelyn agreed, saying, "They will get plenty of negative feedback, so try to be as positive as possible."

There are so many things in this world that can drag us down if we let them. ADHD is certainly on that list for all individuals who have it, and their families. Constantly thinking about ADHD creates a perpetual stream of negativity. Don't get me wrong, ADHD is pervasive and it's hard not to think about it. When your child is first diagnosed, you won't think about much else. It does get easier to push it toward the back of your mind as time goes on though — I promise.

Remaining positive has a direct correlation to your child's self-esteem. Think about it: if you are focusing on your child's positive attributes, that nurtures confidence and reminds them they are more than just their ADHD weaknesses. Mary offers an idea for how to do just that: "Tell your child they are capable, intelligent individuals and able to achieve anything they want."

"My mom always told me I was smart," boasted Colleen. Her mom's instinct was to focus on the positive even though she wasn't diagnosed at the time, not until her fifties.

I tell Ricochet something positive every night when I tuck him in. It usually starts with, "I like the way you..." I try to choose something that he is working on improving that I saw him doing well that day, or I compliment something I love about him...

> "I like the way you let your friend choose the activity when he was at our house today."

> "I like the way you told Momma the truth when the vase was broken."

> "I like the way you said 'Excuse me, please' and then waited for me to finish talking to Daddy before you started talking."

> "I like the way you ate your snack at the table and not in the living room."

> "I like the way you were concerned when your friend was sad and you tried to help her laugh and feel better."

> "I like the way you let me know where you were going before you went outside to play."

Not only does this praise end the day on a positive note for Ricochet, but he usually falls asleep with a smile. I also get a reminder of his strengths and all he does right/well to close my day. This is the simplest little thing really, but it makes a monumental positive impact.

Praise helps kids realize they are capable, and feeling capable builds self-esteem, too. Ella told me, "I suffered from a lot of self-esteem issues because I felt like I was an outcast. No one ever did anything to cause those feelings; it was [my] internal struggle." Many kids with ADHD already feel bad about themselves because of all the negative messages they are bombarded with due to ADHD behaviors. They need their parents to fill the void and focus on their gifts. "Provide as much positive feedback as possible," advises Jake. "Show your child how proud you are of them."

"Do whatever you can to keep your child's confidence up," shared Ingrid, also diagnosed with ADHD as an adult.

Terry Matlen reminded us that a positive outlook is important for teachers, too, when she shared this advice: "Teachers, always point out the positives instead of focusing on the negatives. I don't think teachers realize how much of an influence they are on a child's self-esteem."

Self-esteem is boosted through accomplishment. Your child needs to be reminded, through experiencing actual successful outcomes, that they can meet expectations and achieve other goals set for them, or that they set for themselves. If they don't have frequent opportunities to feel successful at something, they will trudge through life feeling like a failure and give up on trying altogether at some point. Be sure to nurture their talents and interests a great deal — classes, clubs, social gatherings, etc. are a great way to do this.

Support Adds Strength

Always have your child's back, no matter what. Believe in them. Advocate for them!

Believing in your child and always having their back is so important for kids with ADHD, a message I heard again and again from the adults with ADHD who answered the survey. Just as scaffolding adds support to a building, it also adds support for your child to stand on their own two feet.

Be there for them. Love them unconditionally. Help them in areas where they struggle (lagging skills). Advocate for their special needs. Believe in them. Fight for them. Always be in their corner. Scott, a young adult, shared that the best thing his parents ever did for him was "fight in my corner."

"Support, without blame and shame, is so important to deal with ADHD," advised Rick.

Support can take many different forms. "My mom and dad were actively involved in many school and field trip events," shares Eva. "This allowed me to be teased a lot less."

"My parents were very big advocates for me, especially when I was bullied by others," shared Marlow.

"[My parents] knew that homework was very difficult for me, and they did not push too hard," shares Jake.

"They never made me feel guilty about the difficulties I had or the poor grades."

Allowing your child to speak up for themselves and have a part in decisions about them is supportive, too. Ella says, "[My parents were] very supportive of my voice while creating a 504 and IEP plan." Encouraging her to express her needs and backing her up on those requests was not only supportive, but it also taught her to advocate for herself at an early age.

Part of supporting your child is creating structure in their environment. Set expectations and facilitate predictability through daily schedules and routines

Routines, reminders, and limits create the consistency and support to learn self-regulation skills.

Another big area for parents to show their support of their kids with ADHD is in advocating for their special needs at school. Most kids with ADHD are the proverbial square peg in a round hole when it comes to school. Our schools are structured on a group model where two to three dozen kids are expected to all be still, quiet, and attend for hours. Those expectations often aren't realistic for our square-peg kids. That means parents have to advocate for their child's different needs so they have the same opportunities at academic success as the neurotypical (round-peg) kids.

"Never stop advocating for your child," recommends Jill. "There's always a way to figure things out for him/her. Just because it's not the traditional way, doesn't mean it can't work. Never give up."

The survey responders had a good bit of advice in this area when asked to recommend what they feel is most important for kids with ADHD. "Advocate for your children by educating others, and teach them how to advocate for themselves," advises Kim. "To do so, they need to understand at least the 'what' of ADHD so they can understand the 'why' behind everything in their life."

Of course, teachers can be supportive, too. I think it's as important as the support of parents really, especially because the school environment is usually anything but supportive for kids with ADHD. "In junior high, I had a choir teacher that believed in me," shared Eva. "When kids teased me for being 'flaky' (really, I just had an uncanny, out-of-the-box sense of humor), she would make a point to tell me she was the same way. She and my band teacher were huge sources of support."

Rick shares, "[One of my teachers] said she would help me stay focused through some exercises in reading. The acknowledgement, support, and then some action made me feel everything was Ok."

"[One teacher] told me I was talented and more capable than I thought myself to be," offered Samuel.

Tread with caution in the area of supporting a child with special needs, however. There's a fine line between supporting and enabling. Don't be a helicopter parent. Hovering over your child and doing things *for* them only leads to learned helplessness. Instead, offer the support necessary for them to *learn to do things themselves*, grow independent, and gain confidence, but no more.

How can a child believe he can succeed if his teachers and parents don't? Your support is crucial.

Appropriate Expectations Bring Relief

Define Expectations and Encourage Accountability

Imagine a society where there are no rules. Not only would it be the definition of pandemonium and chaos, but it would breed anxiety of the deepest level. You would have no idea if you would be rewarded or punished at any given time. You would be constantly worried and stressed. It would be terrifying! Now, imagine yourself as a child about your own child's age who has no idea what to expect from others.

Kids (and adults) want to know where their boundaries are, whether they realize it consciously or not. They need to see these barrier lines to stay within them to succeed — do the right thing, please others, and meet expectations. With visible, defined boundaries, kids know undoubtedly when they'll be rewarded and when they'll be punished. We have a human need to have clearly defined expectations, and kids aren't immune to that, especially kids with ADHD.

"The best thing my parents did for me was to provide strict, firm boundaries with fair punishments," said Nicole.

That goes for teachers too, as Maggie explained, "The best thing a teacher ever did for me was give me clear instructions on what I needed to know."

Many individuals with ADHD will tell you that they felt it was impossible to meet expectations when they were kids. That feeling haunts many into adulthood, too. This growing feeling is evident in your kids when they make statements such as, "I can't do anything right," "I'm so dumb," or "I'm a bad kid." You can take away a lot of the pain of perceived ineptitude by explicitly defining expectations simply and clearly.

"The thing I need most for my ADHD, and why I did so well in school, is a very clear set of guidelines," shared Kim, "but my parents were also there along the way to serve as bumpers to keep me on course when I was struggling."

I hear you saying that you discuss rules and expectations with your kids, but that activity must look completely different when defining expectations for kids with ADHD.

Don't assume a child with ADHD knows their boundaries for any given task. Yes, sometimes the boundaries are common sense, but common sense isn't always intuitive for a child with ADHD. Furthermore, they often can't read subtle social cues to weigh their influence on these expectations. Don't assume what's obvious is obvious to a child with ADHD. Err on the side of defining too much rather than too little, and you will see the benefits of clearly defined expectations in your family.

The structure of defined expectations removes anxiety and provides room for calm as well. I'll share with you the same visualizing exercise I share in my previous book, *What to Expect When Parenting Children with ADHD*. Imagine you are given a verbal command to stay within "your area." If there's a chalk outline on the floor around you, you feel pretty good that you can stay within that area — you can see where the boundaries are, and you are comfortable with the task. But if you are asked to stay within "your area" and there are no visible boundaries, or instructions to define the boundaries of "your area," you are likely to feel anxious about being able to comply with this task. You may feel paralyzed and not move for fear of crossing the invisible boundary. You will be uncomfortable not knowing if you are successfully working toward your goal or not. The power of clearly defined expectations is noticeably logical.

Parents are guided by the calendar age of their kids when setting expectations for them. When your child has a neurodevelopmental disorder like ADHD, that societal wisdom points your compass too far north.

Kids with ADHD are two to three years behind their peers in maturity and other developmental markers. Age-appropriate expectations are then two to three years ahead of their capability. It's so important to remember that gap when setting expectations and doling out discipline. Our expectations need to be guided by our child's development, not his calendar age.

Discovering the right expectations for your child involves: reading all you can about ADHD and any other conditions he has; documenting and studying his behavior to find patterns and to determine triggers; and learning what motivates him. It's a long process but, until you discover and accept your child's developmental age, you cannot set appropriate expectations.

"My best advice for parents of kids with ADHD is to delay expectations, not lower them," offers Brent, who was diagnosed very young. That beautifully illustrates the difference in expectations due to developmental delay.

Accepting your child's truth has a big effect on his self-esteem, too. If you always ask him to meet expectations that are beyond his capability, he will feel incapable, broken, and misunderstood. Those feelings lead to low self-esteem, anger, outbursts, and other unwanted behaviors.

When you know where your child is in terms of development, you support him, show unconditional love, and boost his self-esteem.

I have worked very hard over the last seven years to discover Ricochet's true developmental age. I know him very well at this point (although he's always changing and there's always more to learn). It took a long time, but I now know what he needs in terms of expectations.

Crisis behaviors — extreme fears, self-harm, lashing out more than usual — occur when expectations are greater than capability. Crisis behaviors are a good sign that your expectations (or the school's expectations) are inappropriate, too high for your child's developmental age. Be proactive and discover and implement appropriate expectations as soon as possible, so you don't experience these troublesome crisis behaviors.

The one exception to the expectation of staying within boundaries? Pushing your own boundaries, Pamela reminds us. "Teach your kids that pushing through and finishing is more rewarding, and that you have a chance to push your own limits and boundaries."

Every Child Has Strengths & Talents

Nurture Talents and Interests to Boost Confidence & Self-Esteem

I had more comments during the ADHD Adult Survey about nurturing strengths than any other category. Those who have succeeded in adulthood feel they can attribute their success to this, at least in part. Those who have struggled in adulthood also attribute much of that to a focus all their lives on their weaknesses, their ADHD. Again and again, survey responders said, "Find your child's strengths and focus on them."

"Let them know that their behavior does not define them," offers Caroline. "I was labeled a 'bad child' for a long time."

It's true — individuals with ADHD have a particular set of weaknesses that make day-to-day life more challenging. They aren't just a collection of weaknesses though. Remind your child often that we all have weaknesses, whether we have ADHD or not. It might go something like this:

> "Did you know Daddy isn't very good at math? Yep, it's true. But you are great at math! We all have things we're really good at and things we're not so good at."

Eva offered an illustration of the support that acknowledging that everyone has weaknesses offers: "In high school, my AP Calculus teacher stood next to me as I sat with tears spilling all over an unanswered test and said, 'It's okay, [Eva], you don't have to be good at everything.'"

We also all have strengths. It's crucial to focus as much attention and awareness as possible on your child's strengths and interests, to overshadow the pervasive weaknesses that are part of ADHD. This is a key ingredient to boost confidence and self-esteem, as Hannah advised:

"Allow [your child] to spend as much time doing what they excel in as they spend on what they struggle with. Never take away the extracurricular activities or special interests they love as a punishment for poor academic grades or an inability to focus. If you do that, they will feel completely lost and become more apathetic."

It's vitally important to have conversations about more than just our child's weaknesses and struggles, whether we are talking to our child directly, to someone else while our child can hear us, or to any others in their lives, even if they're not within earshot. If we spend all our time talking about ADHD, life becomes all about ADHD, and that leaves no room for anything else. As parents of kids with ADHD, it's our responsibility to help them discover and nurture their talents and interests. Self-confidence can't be instilled in an environment where conversations and activities always revolve around ADHD and weaknesses. Prohibit negativity as much as possible.

Make a list of everything good about your child (there's a worksheet for this in my previous book, *What to Expect When Parenting Children with ADHD*). Even the small things count here. Be sure your list includes their strengths, talents, hobbies, aptitudes, positive personality traits, athleticism, interests, etc. Really go the extra mile to fill at least one page. Ask your child to join you and help you fill the list. Talking about their positive traits is one of the very best things you can do for your child.

My list of strengths for Ricochet:

- Kind
- Gentle
- Considerate
- Loyal
- Good at math
- Good at science
- Loves chemistry and physics
- Very smart
- Enormously creative
- Inventive
- Charming
- Good with animals
- Intuitive with technology
- Approachable
- Loves graphic novels
- Great at video games
- Interested in how things work
- Loves to explore
- enacious
- Witty
- Friendly
- Enjoys making others laugh
- Determined

Once you complete your list of wonderfulness, ask your child to help you pick two items on the list that they would like to do more of or learn more about and start there. For instance, if your child is into mechanics and how things work, offer to sign them up for a kid's electrical circuitry class, or purchase a kit for children to experiment with mechanics at home (the website ToysAreTools.com is an excellent resource for toys that are science-based and/or inspire thoughtful play). Or if they're really into working with clay, offer to enroll them in pottery classes, or get some clay and tools for a little home pottery studio. Ricochet has participated in several summer day camps that focused on science and did well with all of them because he is super-interested in the subject matter.

"In elementary school, the best thing my teachers did was recognize the value in having skills in creativity and the arts," shares Eva. "I gained confidence and built self-esteem through my artistic endeavors," she remembers. "My parents started us young, so I had that confidence from a very early age. It probably saved my life, and I know it gave me the confidence and discipline to persevere."

The most helpful thing my parents did for me as a child with ADHD was "focus on my strengths — my gifts and talents," said Terry Matlen, adult with ADHD and author of *The Queen of Distraction*.

When our kids have opportunities to do things well and succeed often, they begin to realize they aren't just "a screw-up," "stupid," "lazy," or any number of other negative things kids with ADHD often think about themselves when they perpetually hear about their weaknesses, or when they can't ever seem to reach the level of their peers. The best thing my family did for me as a child was "Tried to keep me interested in my creative strengths and not focus on my shortcomings," says Keith.

"I had one teacher in tenth grade who looked past my immaturity and saw my talents," offered Lynn. "He surprised me with a one-day college journalism seminar for high school students who basically had extreme potential. I was one of three chosen. I never, ever forgot that. He helped me to believe in myself."

Facilitate excitement about the things your child with ADHD excels in — the rewards will be exponentially greater than the investment and will last a lifetime.

"My parents would let me spend time with other adults who had things I was interested in that we didn't have at home," shared Nicole. "I got to spend time on farms, working with the animals and riding other people's horses. This also allowed me to build relationships with other adults that probably helped greatly with my people skills."

Terry told me, "Though my artistic gifts didn't become apparent until later, my mother really supported my efforts in this area. [When my grades dropped] nothing much was said about all that by my mother, but she praised my artwork up and down, and that helped my self-esteem in a huge way."

And don't worry about quickly changing interests — Diana said the best thing her family did for her was allow her to explore her interests, even though they changed often.

"Really focus on the child's strengths and encourage skill development in his areas of interest," advises Terry, "even if it means he switches to different interests and doesn't stick to one thing."

We can't all know what we're good at, or what we enjoy most, without trying out some things. See it as the journey to figuring out what makes them tick.

Meet Kids Where They Are

Acknowledge and Accept: Be Flexible, Throw Out Traditional Expectations

We demand flexibility of our inflexible children, yet we are rigid in our expectations of those very same children. We must throw out traditional expectations of children their age or gender and accept our kids right where they are, each and every day.

Parents of children with ADHD must recognize and accept that a child with ADHD is developmentally younger than the number of years since they were born. When dealing with a developmental disorder like ADHD, parents have to develop a new frame of reference and meet these kids where *they* are.

For instance, my twelve-year-old son is old enough by traditional standards to handle disappointment without tears and/or an outburst. However, the characteristics of ADHD must be the deciding factor in his ability to effectively handle disappointment — the nuances of ADHD say he can be twelve and not handle disappointment like a twelve-year-old should. By using ADHD as my new frame of reference, I can identify that this reaction to disappointment could very well be typical for my child. If I didn't reframe my perspective, my response would be critical, and not in a constructive manner.

"Realize that trying harder isn't the solution," Lillian offers. "Your child literally *can't* do many of the things you take for granted."

The adults who took the ADHD survey said again and again that they felt constantly criticized growing up. I imagine that's because the adults in their lives weren't meeting them where they were. Audrey shared the impact of validating emotions with me. "Help [kids with ADHD] manage emotions," she recommended. "No one really talks about emotions and ADHD, they only talk about getting distracted, disorganization, etc., but emotions play a big role. I often overreacted to situations, and then I would be labeled 'selfish,' 'over-emotional,' and a 'baby.' I was invalidated and not taken seriously. It had a very big impact on my confidence and willingness to express emotion as I got older. At nineteen, I am now diagnosed, on medication, and seeing a therapist, but I still struggle with my emotions very much and am continuously working through them and understanding that I am valid and that I am important."

A teen responder, Alyssa, advised against comparing your child to yourself: "Understand kids with ADHD and don't tell them about [your experiences], because you are two very different people. If you don't have ADHD, you don't understand people with ADHD, because you can't really imagine and put yourself in our shoes."

Ralph, who was diagnosed young, provided a simple example of meeting children with ADHD where they are: "[My parents] let me eat when I was hungry, not when the rest of my family ate. I was on Ritalin from seven to thirteen years old, and I would not be hungry at the usual times. I remember my mother taking me to McDonald's at around 7 or 8 PM every night because that's when I was very hungry."

When teachers meet kids where they are, it can be a huge relief, too. Jill's story illustrates this so well: "When Jill got something wrong on a test, her teacher suggested she take it home and work on it. When questioned about this, the teacher answered, 'Are you finding the right answer? Will you know what the right answer is when you enter it on the test? Then you showed me [you] learned what the right answer was. What more do I need to see?' I had never felt so relieved and understood in my whole life."

Annabelle offered that the best thing teachers ever did for her as a child with ADHD was, "understand that I was trying and just not quite making it happen."

At the same time, the adults surveyed didn't want to feel like they were broken. They wanted to be accepted and acknowledged for who they are, not as someone who has a "condition" or is somehow damaged. Not viewing themselves as broken or damaged allowed them to see their own strengths and merits, too.

"The most helpful thing my parents did for me as a child was not look at my ADHD as a 'condition' like most of my friends and teachers did," explained Kerri, an adult diagnosed with ADHD in grade school. "They never looked at me and said, 'She behaves this way because she has a condition.' Instead they just saw it as *who I was*. It wasn't a bad thing. It was just part of me. They accepted me for me. ADHD will never go away, and I can accept myself a lot easier because I was never allowed to view myself as having a 'condition,' as if I were ill."

Make sure your child knows they aren't crazy, lazy, or stupid. Show compassion and understanding for their struggles, but give them the support and room to breathe needed to find their own way.

Cooper shared a telling story of what happens when you don't acknowledge your child's ADHD and struggles: "[My parents] were extremely unhelpful. They forever insisted that there was nothing wrong with me and made my school life hell for it. Having parents that were aware and willing to work with me on coping mechanisms would have likely avoided my suicidal tendencies as a child." This is the power of acceptance and meeting your child where *they* are — it's *that* important.

Skills Aren't Always Inherent, but Can Be Taught

Build Lagging Skills

ADHD is a developmental disorder. A developmental disorder is defined in the *Developmental Disabilities Assistance and Bill of Rights Act of 2000* as a chronic disability that is attributable to:

- physical or mental impairment *(check)*,
- begins in childhood *(check)*,
- is likely to continue indefinitely *(check)*, and
- results in the substantial functional limitations of at least three of the following:
    - self-care *(yep)*,
    - receptive and expressive language *(yep)*,
    - learning *(most definitely, yep)*,
    - mobility,
    - self-direction *(yep)*,
    - capacity for independent living, or
    - economic self-sufficiency *(possibly)*.

That, my friends, is also a loose definition for ADHD. And, where there's a developmental disorder, there are lagging skills.

It doesn't necessarily "matter" if we call ADHD a behavioral disorder or a developmental disorder, but recognizing that it's a developmental disability gives parents the appropriate perspective to implement strategies that work for ADHD. One such strategy is to teach the skills our kids are expected to have due to their age but which they are lacking altogether or lagging behind in.

Think about the term "developmental disability." It means that if my twelve-year-old has a developmental disability (he has several of them), his development has not yet reached the twelve-year-old standard benchmark but is somewhere behind that. Kids with ADHD are often two to three years behind their peers in maturity and skill development. In my son's case, that means I'm parenting a boy who is nine, maybe ten, which requires an altogether different parenting approach. Yet, he's expected to have the skills of a twelve-year-old, which requires me to teach the skills he needs but has not yet developed.

The skills adults in the survey identified that they needed help with as children with ADHD are:

- Planning and organizing
- Chunking tasks (breaking tasks down into smaller parts)
- Note-taking
- Time management
- Study skills
- Self-advocacy
- Using strengths to overcome weaknesses
- Self-confidence
- Social skills
- Independence
- Follow-through
- Budget and financial management

- Resilience
- Reigning in impulsivity
- Compensation (coping strategies and work-arounds)

"I had one teacher who taught me how to take organized notes in class, and I have used this [method] in every class ever since," explained Hannah, who was diagnosed with ADHD as a teen. "Being taught executive functioning skills like note-taking, chunking assignments into smaller tasks, and learning how to study was helpful."

One common strategy for teaching all these skills is modeling. Kids watch and emulate their parents and other adults in their lives. They define many of their expectations of themselves and others by observing Mom and Dad. Be cognizant of this as you raise your child with ADHD. Make sure you are setting an example you want them to follow.

Another common strategy in teaching all these skills is voicing your thought processes aloud, even your subconscious thoughts, throughout an action or process. For example, you want to teach your child to plan and schedule their day, and you're working on scheduling soccer practice that evening. Talk through every single incremental step aloud:

> "Okay, Ricochet, we need to get your soccer practice on our family schedule. Tell me, what time does soccer practice start?"

> "Six o'clock," he answers.

"Yes, and where am I going to write 'soccer practice' on the calendar?"

He points to the six o'clock block, and I write it in.

"How long do we need to block out for soccer practice? How long does it last?"

"It's one hour, so fill it in until seven o'clock."

"What else do we need to plan for soccer practice? Can we leave here at six o'clock and be on time for practice?"

"No," he giggles.

"So what else do we need to plan on the schedule and block off?"

"The time it takes to drive to practice."

"Right! And the time it takes to drive home, too. Now, do you need to prepare for soccer practice, or do you just walk out the door just like you are right now?"

"I have to get my uniform on, make a water bottle, and grab my cleats."

"Yes!" I would say. "And how long do you think that will take? Should we write that on the calendar and block off that time, too?"

"Yeah."

"Okay, Buddy. So, what time do you need to start getting ready for soccer practice?"

"5:20?"

"Right!"

That is an excellent example of scaffolding and support to teach skills.

Let's take a look at each skill and how you can teach and instill it in greater detail.

Planning and Organizing

Many adults who took the survey talked about how their parent(s) modeled organization and/or helped them with it by walking them through lengthy projects, providing tools like planners and calendars, or talking out the steps to organization. Many of those who didn't have that support with planning and organization as kids recommended it as their top advice for parents now raising kids with ADHD.

"I'm still struggling with organization now!" offered Joyce. "If someone could set up an official 'what to do today' with prompts, I'd be all set." That is precisely what we need to teach our kids with ADHD to do for themselves.

Rachel advised, "Teach the child specific, concrete strategies to compensate for difficulty with planning, organization, and follow-through."

As someone who is inherently gifted at organization, it was a bit difficult to wrap my head around how one teaches this skill. Scaffolding — talking them through the steps of organization in microscopic detail each time they need to implement it — is the first step. "When you're trying to organize your toys, the first thing you do is sort like things together in separate piles," you might say.

Have your child participate in sorting and sequencing games and activities, such as *Sort It Out! Jr.,* and putting the events in order after reading a story. Sorting and sequencing are two key skills in organization.

Keep a family calendar. This models writing things down in a central location, planning ahead, and time management. Instead of maintaining the calendar on your own, enlist your child's help and walk them through the thought processes.

Establish rules for organization. First you sort; next you assign categories; then you find containers for each, for example. Kids with ADHD do best with simple and detailed instructions, one step at a time. Breaking it down into parts also keeps the task less overwhelming.

Help them prioritize with simple rules. Offer four buckets or bins, each with a description of each level of priority, one being the highest priority and number four the lowest. So, for example, when organizing their bedroom old homework papers from classes they've completed would be the lowest priority item they would find probably, so they'd put it in the number four, the lowest priority bin . Or, when prioritizing schoolwork, the extra credit on the latest science project would go in the lowest priority "bucket" because everything else in the project has to be done first.

Use checklists and routines for recurrent tasks and activities, such as cleaning the guinea pig's cage, mowing the lawn, getting ready for school, getting ready for bed, etc.

Give kids problem-solving games. The process of figuring out a solution helps with the skills needed for planning and organization.

My personal favorite organization tip is the "everything has a home" strategy. In the mind of a super-organized person, like me, every single object really does have a home. If it doesn't, it should, and so a home needs to be created for it. The younger you start with this tactic, the more successful it's likely to be. Working memory can wreak havoc on continued practice of "everything has a home," so try labeling buckets, bins, drawers, and shelves. Keep in mind still, this strategy won't work for everyone.

Teach your kids to make lists and use sticky notes, also. Get them in the habit of writing everything down (or typing or speaking it into a digital list).

Chunking Tasks

It's tough for kids with ADHD to see the parts of a whole — they see the end of the maze, but not each twist and turn along the path to successfully get to the end goal. And a large end goal may be too overwhelming and/or intimidating for them to even get started in the first place. The analogy of a deer in headlights comes to mind. When kids with ADHD have a big/multi-step task, they will likely need help breaking it into smaller tasks or "chunking" it.

Chunking involves breaking the task or project down into sequential steps and/or smaller parts. Chunking also refers to a time-management strategy in which one assigns blocks of time, i.e., chunks, to one particular task. This breaks any task or project into easy, achievable steps. (If they aren't easy and achievable steps for your child, you need to break them down even more, into even smaller steps.) Think of chunking as setting mini goals, in sequential order and possibly on a timeline, to achieve the ultimate, larger goal.

Time chunking and multi-tasking are not friends — chunking will not be a successful strategy if you are also trying to multi-task. The chunks of a project should be broken into no more than forty-five minutes to an hour for neurotypical individuals, so I'd say individuals with ADHD, especially kids, need to stick with chunks of roughly twenty to thirty minutes, max.

The easiest way to chunk a large task is to work backwards from the end goal. Say your child has a science project where he has to turn in an essay and a visual. Your child picks the solar system. Start at the end: they must deliver an essay and a visual—how do they get there? Define the visual. To keep it simple, we will assume a hanging mobile of the solar system with earth, sun, and all planets. Make a supplies list for that and note when you will need the supplies by to have enough time to create the visual and turn it in by the due date. Then ask your child what information they need in order to create an accurate visual. Where will they get that information? When do they need that information by in order to get the appropriate supplies and have enough time to execute the visual? Start at the end and map out each tiny step of the project backwards. You are essentially making a timeline of the project, and each entry on the timeline is one "chunk." Of course, you'll want to perform this process with a calendar as a visual to determine the timeline. You can also draw it out on a traditional timeline if that works better for your child.

When teaching skills, it's important that you don't do the planning and organizing for them. Your child needs to go through the motions, and you are simply there to facilitate, teach the process, and keep it on track.

Note-Taking

Note-taking seems simple, right? Just write down what you hear. However, it's the process that lies beneath that can make that a challenging and tricky task for those with ADHD.

Individuals with ADHD struggle with executive functions, the mental skills that help the brain successfully act on an idea. Executive functioning involves planning, organization, memory, time management, and flexible thinking. Thinking of these five characteristics on a literal level, we can see where the lack of these skills can make many tasks more difficult, but they don't seem involved in note-taking. However, executive functions are used by the brain in a much deeper way.

The act of writing is a very complex process for the brain. When taking notes in a lecture, the brain must first decide what is important enough to write down. That process of prioritization takes both planning and organization. Then, once the brain has decided something is important enough to write down, it must commit what was said (what it needs to write down) to memory. Now the brain has to tell the hand how to write each letter, while keeping the whole of the thought in memory, and also listening to and processing the next part of the lecture, because the teacher doesn't pause after every sentence to make sure students get everything written down.

What can be done to accommodate this challenging and complex neurological process for students with ADHD? The simplest answer is to be sure they are given a copy of the notes, either by the teacher or by a dependable student who is an excellent note-taker.

Kate offered an experience that worked for her: "My best learning experience was with my university statistics professor — she read her notes out loud, wrote them on the board word for word, and then explained it all." This is ideal for students with ADHD but not likely to happen in most classrooms, unfortunately.

Assistive technology can be a huge help when it comes to note-taking as well. Apps like *in Class* allow students to type notes and record the entire audio of the lecture in sync. For example, I'm reviewing my notes on the Civil War in my *in Class* app for my upcoming history quiz. I come across a portion of my notes that is confusing and seems to be missing parts. I can tap that area of my notes in the app, and it will play the audio of that point of the lecture so I can make sense of the incomplete section of my notes. Plus, now my notes are saved all in one digital notebook, no papers to try to keep up with and likely get lost.

While note-taking is a skill that can be taught, it's probably not very realistic to think it can be taught with great success to kids with ADHD who also have executive functioning impairment. In this area, it's best to also teach coping mechanisms and work-arounds such as asking for a copy of the notes, audio recording the lectures, and use of other assistive technologies.

Time Management

Individuals with ADHD often have a poor sense of time, sometimes referred to as "time blindness." They don't know how long a task will take and often underestimate or overestimate. They live in the here-and-now, and anything in the future feels too far away. A poor sense of time leads to poor planning, chronic lateness, procrastination, feeling overwhelmed, and more.

Time management is a classic lagging skill for individuals with ADHD, too, and is one of the executive functions that are often weak. As with all lagging skills, time management needs to be taught and scaffolded for kids with ADHD.

It's important to model time management to teach the skill. For example, plan your schedule together, talking through each and every thought process required. Talk about the time needed to get ready and travel to and from a destination. Show them how to block off this extra time on either side of the event on the calendar. Talk through the thought process of determining if anything needs to be done ahead of time before that event, such as completing paperwork before a doctor's appointment or having a physical done before sports try-outs begin.

Routine is an important tool for kids (and adults) with ADHD. It can be beneficial in learning time management, also. Any tasks that can be done in the same block of time every day should be scheduled that way — walking the dog, brushing teeth, eating lunch, doing chores, etc. The same goes for weekly and monthly tasks. It's going to be easiest to remember and keep track of recurring events when they are scheduled and occur at the same time every day, week, or month.

Make learning time management skills a game of sorts. Challenge your child to beat the clock, or challenge their perceptions of how long something takes by timing it. For example, one of Ricochet's chores is emptying the dishwasher and putting all the clean dishes away. Of course, he hates this chore. He was constantly complaining that it "takes forever," which drove me nuts because I knew it could be done in five minutes or less. So I decided to challenge his perception one particularly trying evening.

"I will prove to you that you can empty the dishwasher in about five minutes," I said after a good thirty minutes of enduring his whining, complaining, and refusing.

"You're just trying to trick me into doing it by telling me it's fast when it's not," he grumbled, arms crossed.

"Nope. I'll prove it," I countered. "We will set a timer for five minutes. As long as you are making a good effort to get it done, I will put away everything left after five minutes are up."

His eyes lit up. He assumed he had just gotten out of a good portion of his chore that night. But I knew better. He put the last dish into the cupboard with seven seconds to spare. Then he looked at me with sheer amazement. His poor sense of time had him convinced he was spending a really long time emptying the dishwasher, but now he knows that task really only takes about five minutes. The complaining and resistance to this chore almost disappeared after that.

Measure the time spent on activities where your child seems to get lost for a long period, such as time on the Internet. If they are spending hours online and don't recognize it, set a stopwatch so they can see how long thirty minutes, an hour, or even two hours feels when playing on the computer.

Experts say analog clocks, the old-fashioned clocks with the hour and minute hands, are best for individuals with a poor sense of time. This way you can see chunks of time and the passage of time on the face of the clock, making time more real. There are some tools and gadgets that can help overcome the poor concept of time, too. My favorite is the Time Timer®. The red disc shows the amount of time it's set for, and it disappears as the time passes.

Time Timer®

Teach your child to use alarms as well, especially with scheduling. Most individuals with ADHD find that setting a couple of alarms for an event ensures they will process the alarms and what they mean and move in the right direction. If your child has a smartphone, they can schedule appointments and travel times and set two alarms for each. When your skills are deficient, technology is often a great fail-safe.

Bob describes how a teacher taught him time-management skills, a system that has helped him overcome ADHD weaknesses all his life: "One teacher explained in detail how to manage time, plan for study and homework time, and include exercise and TV times. We drew up a timetable of *every* waking hour of every day during the week. The timetable included favorite TV shows, and time for meals, walking to and from school, jogging in the evenings, etc. Everything [went on the] timetable. I had a page for every week, and this became my diary. Most students had a weekly timetable with only their classes on it, [but our class was taught to consider everything]. If there was a change during the week, I could quickly rearrange things to fit it in without missing important study, especially assignments. I did study and homework for about forty hours — yes forty! — a week and went to school as well. This won me a scholarship."

There is a planner that implements this method of scheduling everything, not just school-related tasks, available for purchase now. It's Order Out of Chaos's Academic Planner.

Study Skills

Some people are born with the fundamental ability to organize notes and information for studying, as well as the motivation to actually do it simply because it's important. Most individuals with ADHD are not; therefore, study skills have to be taught.

Study methods must be tailored to each individual's strengths, weaknesses, interests, and learning style. For example, flash cards might work for one student who thrives on trying to beat the clock and is an auditory learner, but the pressure to know each card's answer in an instant could be too much stress for another student and not visual enough.

Use your child's strengths and learning style to help them craft and learn effective study skills. You will need to work closely with your child throughout the process to ensure they learn and implement successful skills. Be sure to also praise and reward their creating and sticking to their study plan.

First, start with some basic study rules:

- **Believe in yourself.** The more confident children are, the better they will perform typically. Encourage a positive attitude.
- **Eliminate distractions**, including their phone and other electronics. The exception to this rule is for kids who focus better with music or noise in the background. SimplyNoise.com is a free tool for background noise, if needed.
- **Don't wait until the day before** a quiz or test to study. Break it down into smaller chunks and study a little bit each day. (Parents should help with this process until your child can do it effectively on their own.)
- **Study when most alert.** This time of day or night will be different for everyone, but it could be before school, after school, or even at 2 AM, if that's what works for that individual student.
- **Develop a study routine**, i.e., same place, same time. Ricochet does his homework at the breakfast bar at 4 PM each weekday. We strive for the same place and time every day, and the routine reduces (not cures) whining about homework.

Following are some study method ideas. The greatest success comes from using multiple study methods:

- Watch videos on the material being studied on sites like KhanAcademy.com and YouTube.com. (Parents: be mindful of what your kids are watching on YouTube.com and watch over them while on YouTube.com.)

- Quiz with flashcards (write them on index cards or use a flashcard app on a smartphone or tablet).
- Quiz by themselves or by another, or even online on websites like KhanAcademy.com.
- Read and reread the material. (Reading aloud is often helpful for retention, too.)
- Reread and highlight notes and use different colors to categorize what is highlighted. (Ask the teacher for the notes if your child is not a good note-taker.)
- Use the star method to ensure that each section has been reviewed enough — each time the student reviews a section of notes, they draw a star in the top-right corner of the page and date it. When it has five or more stars, the student should have good comprehension and retention of that section of material.
- Write or speak a summary of the material.
- Describe the material to someone, as if the student is teaching them brand-new material they've never heard.
- Put the material to music and sing it.
- Create an outline, graphic organizer, or diagram of the material — start with the main ideas, then add supporting details and sub details.
- Write down what they know on the subject from memory again and again until they are confident they know the material.
- Create memorable analogies, acronyms, anagrams, etc.
- Review returned assignments where mistakes have been corrected.

- Answer study guide questions.
- Form a study group with others studying the same material.
- Focus the most energy on the parts of the material not understood.
- Take breaks when needed (a good time for a snack and a stretch).
- Add body movement while studying: pacing, jumping rope, sit-ups, dancing, running in place, etc., even yoga.

For kids in middle or high school, having a study hall in their schedule is ideal, as Dorothy shared: "Taking a study hall allowed me to get more help on material I didn't understand and gave me more time to study."

Self-Confidence

"Confidence is the number one thing I wish I could have had more of growing up," said Martin, diagnosed in early elementary school. "Now I'm trying to catch up, eliminate the thoughts that make me feel incompetent, and believe in myself."

Parents are the main source of a child's sense of self-worth when they are young. It's part of our job to raise confident children. We do that by showing our kids they are valuable — to us and to the world around them. There are many ways to help our kids build confidence.

Giving your time to your child is one way to show them they are valuable to you. Kids know adults are busy and have many things on their list of responsibilities.

When a parent spends time with their child, that child knows that it's a sacrifice in one way or another. And they know you made that sacrifice because you feel they are important. Leave the dirty dishes in the sink for an hour and play a board game or ride bikes with your child.

Model self-confidence. Kids learn a lot from their parents, including how to value themselves. If you are walking around down on yourself all the time, you're inadvertently teaching your child to be down on themselves, too, teaching them that's what people do. I'm as guilty of this as the next momma — I do not have a good body image, and I make far too many remarks about it in front of my children. That's a work in progress for me. I need to show my kids that we all have value, just for different reasons.

Don't focus on labels. Yes, your child has ADHD, but you can't say your child "is ADHD." There are so many facets to each of our kids, and ADHD is just one of them. Talking all the time about ADHD only focuses your child and the whole family on the negative. Keep things positive and build confidence by focusing on strengths, interests, and talents instead. Remember, every child has strengths and talents; focus on those.

Offer opportunities for success, lots of them. Success builds competence, which is crucial to self-esteem. That feeling of accomplishment when they reach the end with success is a big confidence booster. The more they feel accomplished, the better their self-esteem.

"Both of my parents emphasized the importance of arts education (i.e., music, dance, fine arts, and drama), which is where I truly shone," shared Eva. "I gained confidence and built self-esteem through my artistic talents and endeavors. And they started young, so I had that confidence from a very early age. It probably saved my life, and I know it gave me the confidence and discipline to persevere."

A note of caution about offering opportunities for success: remember to base activities on your child's *developmental* age, not their calendar age, to give them opportunities for success. If you choose activities outside their skill level, you are only setting them up for failure and a hit to their self-esteem.

Let your kids figure things out on their own. Put your pilot's license away and stop hovering. I finally learned a couple of years ago that my propensity for helicopter parenting to protect my kids was actually doing more harm than good. If we do everything for our kids, they never learn to do for themselves. There's a sense of accomplishment and pride when a child does things for themselves. And when we protect our kids from failure, we rob them of the opportunity to problem-solve and the reward of figuring it out on their own. Take a step back to build your child's confidence.

You don't have to take such a large step back that your child is at risk though. Marshall offers, "My mother gave me choices to build my confidence." This is the first step to teaching independence and problem solving.

Help your child find their tribe. Kids with ADHD often feel like outcasts or like they don't fit in. Yet, acceptance is a crucial part of building self-confidence. Offer your children opportunities to discover and spend time with kids who understand and accept them. This could be participation in something like scouts or team sports or even a gaming club. Find a way for your child to spend time with kids with the same interests, and the social comradery and acceptance will help their confidence.

Lastly, make sure your child knows that you believe in them. Offer a healthy dose of "atta boy" or "atta girl" and encouragement. Let your child know you have faith in them. This really works, as evidenced by Scott who said, "My parents believed in me, which gave me confidence."

Social Skills

"Help them build healthy friendships," advised Mary. "Social skills are so important for success and happiness." We think about social skills only in terms of their consequence on friendships and other relationships, but good social skills are integral to success in the workplace, too, or even when checking out at the grocery store. In part at least, social skills can make or break success.

Successful social interactions can be few and far between for kids with ADHD though. Their heightened activity level and abundant enthusiasm often overwhelm their peers. They may not be good at reading nonverbal communication, like body language and tone of voice. And they often manage to interrupt and monopolize conversations without intending to.

The good news is that effective social skills can be taught. Practicing various social interactions with your child will help them learn how to handle specific situations in socially acceptable ways, which will improve their social interactions. Practice how to join a group activity, how to respectfully join a conversation, how to react to teasing or bullying, how to interact with others in public, etc.

Working on reading nonverbal communication cues will be helpful, too. Review different facial expressions and what they mean. Speak to your child in different tones and have them interpret the emotions. Also practice making inferences, a critical social skill for successful relationships with peers in the preteen years and beyond. For example, preteen boys tend to say negative things to each other to signify some sort of comradery — give your child examples of what someone might say and have them tell you what the person meant, or what their intention was, to practice making inferences.

Some children will even need to learn scripts for different situations. For example, if your child is awkward when meeting someone new, teach them to say, "My name is ____. What is yours?" and then to ask a question about the other person. In the end, they should say "It was nice to meet you" or something similar. These pleasantries are essential to successful social interaction and the prospect of repeated interactions with the same individuals.

If you're not having much luck at home with building social skills, look for a social skills group in your area (often part of autism services), or have your child work with an occupational therapist or speech pathologist on these skills.

Remember, it's not the number of friends one has that makes people happiest, it is the quality of the friendships and relationships. Focus on helping your child build quality interactions and friendships, not a large group of friends.

Independence

The first step to independence is learning to do things on your own. Make a conscious effort to step back and let your child take the reins, even if the task will take longer or be messier when your child does it all on their own. The only way to learn to do for yourself is to actually do it.

The parent's role in teaching independence is to monitor the situation and provide support, if needed. Remember, our kids need lots of opportunities for success to build their fragile self-esteem. The pride gained by successfully doing things on their own is great for that.

Chores are a great way to start teaching kids with ADHD independence. By your assigning responsibility and stepping back, your child learns that it is sometimes their responsibility to take care of things on their own and that they can succeed at it. They may need more time and more instruction, but they can learn independence.

When kids are younger, start teaching some independence by offering measured choices. If you tell your six-year-old they can wear whatever they want to school, they might meet you at the door in their swimsuit, snorkel mask, and flippers, despite the six inches of snow on the ground. However, if you offer two or three appropriate options, you're allowing them to make the decision but in a controlled way. This is the first step to teaching kids with ADHD independence.

Older kids need to learn to advocate for themselves as well. Once they finish high school, parents can no longer advocate on their behalf. If they're going to attend college, they have to know how to discern what they need and go to the right people and ask for it. Many a kid with ADHD with helicopter parents has fallen flat on their face at this very intersection of life. Make sure your child is ready when the time comes by having him participate in school meetings as early as he's ready. This is another piece of independence that they need to succeed.

Ask yourself where you can step back to give your child the opportunity to step up and do it.

Follow-Through

Individuals with ADHD crave novelty, as it's very stimulating. This often means that tasks, activities, or projects become boring, and the individual with ADHD loses interest before completion. There are some coping skills you can teach your child to compensate for this.

Start by chunking the task into smaller pieces then schedule every step, complete with reminders. Scheduling it like this, on paper or in a digital calendar, makes it a bit harder to give up on before reaching the finish line, and it makes the task or project feel more manageable. Teach your child to schedule "boring" tasks at a time of day when they have more energy. This will create a much greater likelihood that they won't be able to use being tired or drained as an excuse to procrastinate. Show your child how to write down each step on a sticky note and leave the notes where they can't be missed. Advise them to set more than one reminder so it cannot be ignored.

Be sure to define the end goal. Even if the goal itself isn't motivation for your child with ADHD, there will still be a sense of accomplishment from achieving a goal. And that warm, fuzzy feeling of accomplishment can be addictive.

Don't allow for incremental steps when unnecessary. For example, it's your child's responsibility to get the towels out of the dryer, fold them, and put them away in the linen closet. Rather than move the towels from the dryer to a laundry basket to fold later, where the towels may reside for who knows how long, fold each towel as it's removed from the dryer.

Instill the rule that you cannot start a new task or project until you finish the one you're currently on. Novelty can be a huge distraction and draw an individual with ADHD away from what they have become bored with but must complete. Make the reward for following through to completion the excitement of the novelty of the next project.

Lastly, teach your child when it's Ok to quit before completing something. If one takes on too much, nothing will ever get finished. Our kids have to learn how to prioritize and only take on what they can handle, but they also have to be able to discern when it's acceptable to not see something through to completion. It's Ok to quit when it becomes apparent that you cannot be successful at an activity — I allowed Ricochet to quit baseball before the season was over one year because it was obvious baseball just wasn't for him, and he wasn't doing anything but distracting the coaches and players and warming the bench. It's also Ok to quit something if continuing creates hardship (financial or emotional).

Budget and Financial

It's no secret that individuals with ADHD struggle with money management. It taps into those same lagging executive functioning skills like prioritizing, planning, organization, and memory. Spending too much or buying things you don't need is also an easy pitfall of impulsivity. Mary advised, "Teach them about money management early — budgets, savings, and taxes. They will be better off when they enter the adult world."

My husband does not have an ADHD diagnosis, but we feel pretty certain he has ADHD. After only a couple of months of marriage, it became apparent that I would have to manage the purse strings in our household because I have more developed planning and organizational skills. Unfortunately, he was never taught money management skills, and he wasn't born with them.

If your child with ADHD (all your children really) has the opportunity to take a personal finance class, I strongly recommend it. We required our daughter to take this class in high school, and we will require Ricochet to do the same once he's eligible. All kids need to learn successful money management skills, but it's especially important for kids with ADHD, since little if any of it is inherent.

A weekly allowance is a great way to teach kids money management skills, as well. Teach them to think of their allowance just like a paycheck. When they show up and take care of their responsibilities, they earn their pay. Help them learn to distinguish needs from wants and resist impulse buys. I ask my son to wait 48 hours sometimes before making a purchase when I think he won't care about the item for very long — if he still has it on his mind and still thinks he really wants to spend his money on it, then he can. So often he forgets all about that item — it was just the excitement of the moment. Teach your child how to comparison shop for things they want, too. Walk them through researching the price at different retailers and choosing the best bang for their buck.

Another way to teach kids financial planning and responsibility is to have them help you pay the bills. I don't mean that they contribute their money to paying the bills, I mean that they sit with you and go through the motions as you pay the family bills. This way, they see how much everyday living expenses cost, how to manage and prioritize bills, and how to write checks and log money going in and out, or how to use online bill pay.

When your child is old enough, maybe when they start working, help them create their own budget and set up their chosen money management system. Have them do it, but be there to advise and facilitate and lend your wisdom where needed (and welcome).

Resilience

"Being happy is not about comfort or progress," writes Mantu Joshi in his book, *The Resilient Parent*. "It has everything to do with acceptance and peaceful living." Growing up with ADHD is stressful. Our kids can let it bring them down, or they can find acceptance and learn to be resilient and bounce back from difficult situations. Resilience is one key to success and happiness when you have ADHD. Fortunately, resilience can be taught, encouraged, and reinforced.

Here is yet another reason helicopter parenting is a big no-no. As with many of the skills I've covered thus far, kids cannot learn resilience if their parents are overprotective and seek to prevent every discomfort for their kids. How can you learn to bounce back from a tough situation if you never experience a tough situation? You simply can't. Teach your child to see struggles as challenges to overcome or problems to solve.

Resilience is another skill that is learned, in part, through failure and distress. Allow your child appropriate risks and opportunities to problem-solve on their own. Facilitate this process by talking it through with them and asking many questions to help them come to their own solutions.

If your child has a lot of anxiety, for instance, ask them how they might handle a feared situation if it were to come true. Ricochet started seventh grade this year at a fairly large school that was new to him. He had some anxiety about getting overwhelmed in the hallway and not getting to class on time and/or prepared. So I asked him, "What will you do if you get overwhelmed in the hallway between classes?" His idea was to seek the help of his special education teacher, which was a great solution. To further reiterate that he had a plan, that he could bounce back from this discomfort if it happened, we talked with his special education teacher about this plan at Meet the Teacher, the day before school started. Making this connection with another person, someone to lean on when in distress, is another strategy of resilience. Ricochet came up with a plan to get back on track, and he confirmed it with those who would need to support it. These are the steps to resilience, folks.

Managing emotions is another key component of resiliency. It's healthy to be emotional when struggling or under stress. Kids with ADHD need help to learn how to appropriately manage and work through these emotions. In the example above, I could add a statement to Ricochet such as, "It's OK to get anxious or stressed in the hallway between classes — it's loud and crowded and that makes you uncomfortable. What's important is doing something about it rather than letting your emotions overtake you. Talking with your special needs teacher is a good strategy to manage your emotions in that situation."

Taking a break and time for some self-care is another strategy of resilient individuals. Work with your child on recognizing when they need a break and advocating for themselves to get that break. For example, Ricochet is overwhelmed by the worksheet he has to complete during math class. He gets started and works a couple problems, but feels he will never finish. He feels like he wants to give up and just not try if he cannot succeed. He needs a break now and it's up to him to ask for it. Be sure your child knows to be very clear about *why* they need a break, too. Just telling the math teacher he needs to walk around and get a drink while everyone else is working diligently in their seats likely isn't enough. He needs to also express that he feels overwhelmed and like he might not get finished, so he needs the break to chill so he can refocus. You can practice this through role-playing with your child at home.

A positive outlook is essential to resilience, too, and is another strategy you can model for your child. Having faith and hope that things can get better is essential to bouncing back from adversity or a troubling situation. If you don't think things can get better, you have no purpose to move toward. Teaching our kids to know every tough situation will pass is essential to building resilience. One of my favorite quotes to illustrate this is from *Anne of Greene Gables*. Anne says, "Tomorrow is a new day with no mistakes in it." That's how she talked herself through adversity, and it can work for kids with ADHD as well.

Determination and perseverance are great building blocks for resilience, and kids with ADHD often have both in abundance. All the truths we discussed in the beginning of this chapter, the truths that fall under understanding and positive parenting, boost resilience in our kids, too.

Reining in Impulsivity

Impulsivity, and all its consequential baggage, is reduced only when one thinks through a situation before acting. But those who are clinically impulsive, like our kids with ADHD, tend to do the opposite: act before they think. We cannot change their brains, so how do we change their propensity for impulsivity?

Practicing mindfulness — a focused awareness of one's thoughts and feelings — is one way to challenge impulsive behaviors before acting. Practicing mindfulness can teach your child to take a few seconds to connect with their thoughts before taking action, to hear their inner dialogue. It is becoming a popular complement to ADHD treatment for just this reason. Dr. Mark Bertin's book, *Mindful Parenting for ADHD: A Guide to Cultivating Calm, Reducing Stress & Helping Children Thrive*, is great to learn how to implement mindfulness in the lives of families with a child with ADHD.

Another way to combat impulsivity is to get into the habit of writing thoughts and ideas down first. Just the physical action of writing down what you're feeling or thinking before acting provides time to reflect before proceeding. Sometimes, too, seeing an idea on paper helps you see how silly, inappropriate, or risky it is. Words on paper are not as easy to dismiss as our thoughts are.

Praise your child's decisions and actions that are considerate and well thought-out. This reinforces the desirability of thinking things through before acting, the alternative to impulsivity.

Compensation

There is no cure for ADHD. It cannot be "fixed," no matter how much parents everywhere try. Therefore, kids have to learn to live with ADHD and thrive despite it. "Work on things your child can change and help them compensate for and accept things they can't," offers Leslie.

"Help [your] child set up systems that work for him/her rather than letting them fend for themselves," recommends Jessica, who was not diagnosed until her thirties. The biggest role parents play in compensating for ADHD is providing scaffolding and support for weaknesses and lagging skills, just as she suggests.

"Although I wasn't diagnosed until recently, as an adult," Eva shared, "my mom instinctually picked up on what areas I needed assistance in, e.g., breaking down tedious tasks, planning and organizing lengthier school projects, etc." Having a good support system through family and friends is a great way to compensate for ADHD.

Many responders supported this saying:

"My parents were patient with me and helped me organize my thoughts."

"My mother was very organized, and she helped keep me organized."

"My parents taught me to clean my room and organize it, and they required me to do so bi-weekly."

Many also wished they had been offered more support from parents and/or teachers:

"I wish my parents would have found out the reason for my behaviors and taken action."

"Teach them how to manage the challenges."

"Offer academic, social, and family support."

"Encourage success and help them devote the same dynamics in their weaker areas."

Be careful not to confuse support with doing things *for* your child though. They will not learn to do for themselves if you step in and take over where they are weak. "It helped that my mom was my constant reminder," said Susan, a young adult diagnosed as a preteen, "but life was much harder in college and after without her reminders." She is a classic example of how doing for our children creates learned helplessness. If her mom had taught her how to create her own system for reminders, she probably would have fared better in that area after she left home. Remember, offer ideas and support, but don't do it for them.

The most common type of compensation kids with ADHD experience is accommodations at school. The adults who completed the survey mentioned a variety of accommodations that they found very helpful growing up.

"Concurrently with my parents, the school psychologist, and school staff, I was taught how to work with my distractedness," said Dorothy. "I had an assignment book into which I wrote my homework. At the end of the day, my classroom teacher checked my list and made sure that I had the correct books to get my work done."

A total of four of the ninety-five adults who completed the survey said they found it very helpful when teachers provided extra tutoring or additional help during or after school when they struggled.

Remember Bob and the teacher who taught him a detailed plan to manage time for everything, not just studying and homework? That extra tutelage earned him a scholarship for the last two years of high school and helped him throughout his life.

"My math teacher would keep asking me if I understood what he was trying to teach, and often I didn't," shared Nicole, "and then he would help me work it out."

Another method of compensation for those with ADHD is to create individualized systems and strategies for personal areas of weakness, and many survey responders recommended this. "Learn how your child takes in information and how they give back information," offers Wanda. "Then help them translate that in ways the school system and work world will accept." This is basically discovering and using one's learning style to their advantage. Most individuals with ADHD learn and work best visually (seeing), tactilely (touching), or kinesthetically (moving). Figure out how your child best receives, processes, and distributes information and use that in as many coping strategies as possible.

"Do what you can to help make their world less overwhelming," offered Jake. "Set up systems to help them stay organized and keep a consistent schedule."

Samantha said, "I knew I had trouble finishing my homework, so I asked for strategies. Have a plan for the kids who struggle with concentration. It must be clearly spelled out and is not a license to run wild and free, but a strategy to help get them on track." She makes a good point — accommodations and coping strategies are meant to level the playing field, not to enable your child to use ADHD as an excuse.

More compensating strategies recommended include:

- Opt to take a study hall for one elective to get help with something that is difficult.
- Personal guidance at school with studies and grades.
- See a psychologist for social/relationship and self-esteem issues.
- Parent involvement creating needed structure regarding sleep, personal hygiene, diet, and other elements of a healthy lifestyle.

An ADHD coach is a great tool for creating tailored and effective compensation strategies, specific to how the ADHD brain works and your child's specific strengths and weaknesses. A good behavioral therapist knowledgeable about ADHD can help with this as well.

Accommodations Provide Fairness, Not Destroy It

Accommodations for special needs kids are meant to even the playing field so they have the same opportunities for success as their peers. On the periphery, accommodations often seem unfair to neurotypical classmates (and their parents). Accommodations, such as extended time on tests and reduced assignments, *seem* to many to be an unfair advantage for special needs kids, but they're certainly not.

Diane Malbin, a clinical social worker and Executive Director of FASCETS, offers my favorite definition of fairness:

> "Fair doesn't mean we all get the same thing; fair means we all get what we need."

Accommodations to address the weaknesses of kids with special needs means they get what they need, and that is only fair. No one questions accommodating the special needs of an individual in a wheelchair, so why are accommodations questioned for those with learning handicaps? They certainly shouldn't be. Just because the special needs of kids with ADHD are invisible, it doesn't make them imaginary.

Many of the adults who completed the survey listed accommodations as the most helpful thing a parent or teacher did for them when growing up with ADHD. They mentioned accommodations like tutoring in their weakest subjects, reduced assignments, help with organization, extended time, and making corrections. These opportunities allowed them to feel successful, where without them, they couldn't succeed and would likely have had a negative, detrimental self-image.

Here are many personal stories of accommodations and how beneficial they were for many with ADHD:

"Getting me extra help in math was the best thing my parents did for me when I was a kid."

"[My parents] worked out an arrangement with my teachers where I would do homework for three hours then skip anything left after that."

"A teacher in college once allowed for people who had difficulty answering questions when called on without warning to tell her ahead of time that it was a challenge. This way, I was able to focus better and not spend the whole class in a state of anxiety."

"The best thing a teacher did for me was give me extra time on exams."

"The most helpful thing teachers did for me was provide organizers! All sorts, for essays, for desks. That was such a huge help."

"[Teachers] allowed me many chances to finish my work, even if I didn't turn it in on time."

"[Some teachers] understood that I was actually trying and that I needed extra time."

"I had one teacher who would not give me a hard time or punishment if I was late for homeroom. He gave me a little wiggle room, and it made the year so much better."

"One teacher moved me to the front of the class. This reduced the distractions, and I went from near last to near best in class at about age twelve."

"What helped me was fast beat music while I studied and lots of color and highlighting. Colored drawings of information I needed to remember were very helpful."

"My teachers used a system of Five Minute Warnings when we were working on projects or assignments in class. Those warnings pulled my attention back to the task at hand. My junior and high schools had a buzzer that sounded two minutes before the end of class. That gave us enough time to gather our books and things and get ready for leaving the room to head to our next class."

"One teacher let me have extra time on assignments, even though ADHD was unheard of back then."

"Allowing me to turn in work I had forgotten the day before or reminding me of a weekly assignment I often forgot about by the time it was due was a big help. I had a huge problem with feeling too rushed at the end of classes to put my notes and papers away properly, too. It resulted in a lot of lost notes and homework. Two extra minutes would have made a world of difference in that realm. A 'warning' that things are about to change and get hectic is a big deal for someone with ADHD."

"She would read her notes out loud, wrote it on the board word for word, and then explained it all."

"The best thing a teacher did for me was helped me get engaged in the lesson."

"[Teachers] let me rock my chair back."

"In 4th and 5th grade, my school was one of the first in my area to have a special education program, and they had a special area in the classroom for us ADHD kids (there were five of us in the program, all boys). We weren't segregated from the other kids, we were included in all classroom activities, and we received extra assistance and help in learning when we needed it. I have to say that my teachers then were very supportive and helpful to us, and they went out of their way to be the best teachers I ever had, even though they had little training in LD teaching methods. Thank you very much, Mrs. Hodge and Miss Weber — forty years later!"

"My advice to parents would be to make sure that their child is getting the help they need at school. I wish my teachers didn't just let me get away with not paying attention because I would miss out on the learning, and that's not fair."

Ricochet has had different accommodations over the last seven years in school, but there are some basics that are beneficial to most kids with ADHD, including many of those shared by the Adult ADHD Survey responders above.

In elementary school, asking a child with ADHD-hyperactive type to sit still for long periods of time will not be successful. Permission to wiggle and move about is important for a child with ADHD with hyperactivity. Ricochet's first grade teacher placed a rectangle on the floor around his desk with masking tape — when his peers were expected to attend quietly in their seats, Ricochet was permitted to move about his area as defined by the tape. He could lie on the floor under his desk to do his work, as long as his body and his belongings were within the taped rectangle.

Modified assignments is another important potential accommodation. A child with learning disabilities should only be expected to work as long as their neurotypical peers on homework. The length of time they invest is where there should be equality, not the volume of the workload. This applies to kids with ADHD of all ages if ADHD slows down their efficiency (due to distractibility and/or slow processing speed). Ricochet has a processing speed disproportionate to his IQ (processing is measured as part of many IQ tests), so he cannot complete the same volume of work in the same time as his neurotypical peers — and definitely not as quickly as his IQ score might suggest. If this is a problem for your child as well, ask for modified assignments.

Extended time is also a common accommodation for students with ADHD and goes hand-in-hand with modified assignments. If your child has difficulty with completing tasks in the same time frame as their peers, or if they struggle with overwhelming anxiety under an impending deadline, ask for an extended time accommodation. This will allow them to take their time to do a good job, but will also accommodate for needing extra time due to distraction or poor processing speed.

Ricochet's therapist suggested he have access to a quiet area at school for completing work if he found himself distracted, and that's a good idea for all kids with ADHD. This could be a desk with a study carrel on top, a beanbag in the far corner of the classroom, or a separate room entirely.

Ricochet was also allowed to chew gum in school as an accommodation to improve focus and satisfy his extensive oral-sensory needs. Studies have shown that chewing gum improves focus and academic performance,[xxv] and the U.S. military often provides it to soldiers for that reason. I had to get special permission from the principal, and then it was placed on his official list of accommodations. It was a big help with his obsessive sensory need to chew on something.

Of course, there are dozens more possibilities for classroom accommodations for students with ADHD. Here are some examples:

- Seat student near teacher and/or positive role model.
- Place extra space between desks.
- Provide visual aids.
- Check student agenda for accuracy at the end of each class or school day.
- Provide notes from teacher or peer who is an effective note-taker.
- Provide written, simple, step-by-step instructions.
- Check in with student to ensure instructions were understood.
- Help student get started on independent seat work.
- Offer extra help/tutoring.
- Don't grade for neatness.
- Give exams orally.
- Use assistive technology, such as typing assignments and read aloud e-books.
- Mark in book instead of bubble sheet.
- Offer an extra set of textbooks to keep at home.
- Provide consistent and immediate feedback.
- Use goal-oriented, positive behavior supports instead of punishments.
- Don't withhold recess from student as a consequence.
- Use nonverbal cues, like hand signals, to get the student back on track.
- Allow periodic breaks for movement and refocusing.
- Help with transitions by warning the student of upcoming changes in focus.
- Discuss behavior in private to prevent embarrassment and/or shaming.

- Break assignments into shorter segments by giving the student one shorter portion at a time by folding the paper so only a portion is visible.
- Remind the student to turn in homework when it's due, even if it's a class expectation that they turn it in on their own.
- Allow fidgeting through fidget objects, like stress balls or tactile input, or by allowing the student to doodle.
- Stipulate a "cooling off" area and allow the student to retreat to that location when needed.
- Modify the way assignments are completed to take advantage of the student's learning style. E.g., a visual learner could make a PowerPoint presentation instead of writing an essay.
- Use timers to help the student keep track of the time allotted to complete their assignment and to encourage focus.
- Allow the student to decide what writing style they are most comfortable with, printing or cursive.
- Prompt appropriate social behavior and teach social skills to the student. (This can be in collaboration with school guidance counselors, who sometimes have social skills groups.)

Think about what accommodations might help your child in the classroom, and then propose those items as potential accommodations to the teacher, IEP team, or even the principal. The accommodations list will look different for every child with ADHD, as illustrated by all the different experiences and suggestions the adults who took the survey shared.

Truly Listen to Your Child's Truth

All the input from adults with ADHD that I've talked about thus far leads me to one overarching conclusion: when your child has ADHD, it's paramount to _discover, listen to, and accept_ **_your child's truth_**.

"Parents, really listen to your child," Terry Matlen shares. "I felt my parents were too busy to really sit down and try to understand me."

"Listen, listen, listen to your child," pleads Mary.

"Spend more time listening and less time scolding and making accusations," adds Melissa, "so you don't damage your child's confidence and self-esteem."

"My mom sat in the kitchen and waited for us to come home from school," explained Colleen. "She listened to me every day as I told her about my day."

Each child with ADHD is different, and they are each going to have a different way of doing things. That doesn't make their way wrong, it's just different. And different is OK. Different is to be celebrated even. "Let your child be him/herself all the time. Kids with ADHD are very special in their own way, and to intrude on the way they are is a big mistake," says Ralph. "Let them be kids the way they want to be, not the way _you_ want them to be. My parents were like that for me, and I am totally comfortable being who I am."

Your child may not be telling you the facts of the situation all the time — i.e., lying — but this is not a character flaw or a measure of morality and ethics. When kids with ADHD embellish the truth or tell stories, they are telling you how they interpreted an event or how it *felt* to them — they are telling *their* truth. That is a vital perspective for parents. Don't dismiss what they are saying just because you know it's not one hundred percent factual. Recognize that what they are saying has hidden truth to it — the truth about how they *felt*.

When your son flings open the door with great gusto, marches in from school in the afternoon, and tells you that a classmate "almost killed him" on the playground today, don't interrupt and don't dismiss him. Listen and acknowledge how that felt to him. "That must have really frightened you, Ricochet. I'm sorry that happened." While he wasn't likely almost killed on the playground in a literal sense, that's how it *felt* through his unique and hypersensitive perspective. Saying that a classmate almost killed him on the playground today is *his truth*.

Whatever it may be, this is *your child's* truth, and you have to show them how important their truth is to you in order to nurture trust and respect and to successfully support their needs. One activity I like that will make your child feel truly heard is to write down their concerns with pen and paper. You wouldn't believe how much of a difference it makes in your child's anxiety and stress to simply get pen and paper and write down their concerns. Take it a step further and write down the plan to handle their concerns, too. This made a world of difference when Ricochet was uncomfortable at school and refusing to go.

By writing down what was making him uncomfortable, and then writing up a plan of what we were going to do about each item, he felt we could improve the situation, while just talking about it didn't relieve his anxiety much at all.

There's some background work you must do first before you can successfully identify and determine *your child's* truth. You must learn all you can about ADHD and the unique differences of your child. You must accept that, as Ross Greene, author of *The Explosive Child*, says, "Kids do well if they can." If they aren't doing well with something, find out why. This will only help strengthen your ability to listen to your child's truth. My previous book, *What to Expect When Parenting Children with ADHD*, will walk you through getting to know your child and their differences and behavior triggers. If you haven't reached the point of truly knowing your child in this way yet, I encourage you to work through that book — you will likely have many ah-ha moments.

Your child's truth should be defined by their individual characteristics and needs, strengths and weaknesses, not by their diagnosis. For instance, in general, children with ADHD have a hard time sitting and focusing on one thing for long periods. However, if they are really interested in something (like playing Minecraft), they can sit for hours and attend to it. So, one small piece of Ricochet's truth is that he can focus for hours on Minecraft and other video games he really likes. Another piece of his truth is that he cannot sit still and focus on a school lecture on prepositional phrases or anything that has to do with writing, but he will certainly try to. As

Marlow said when asked what advice she would offer parents raising kids with ADHD today, "Please don't let the diagnosis define what your child is capable of." Be mindful of this trap so you can celebrate the positive aspects of your child's truth.

Melissa summed up "listening to your child's truth" so succinctly, saying the best thing her parents did for her was, "Let me be myself."

I cannot express in words how powerful it can be to discover, listen to, and accept your child's truth. Ricochet at school this year (7th grade) is a prime example. Ricochet has struggled in school horrendously over the years (read *Boy Without Instructions* for all those stories). He is wicked smart, but struggles with attention, executive functioning, writing, inflexibility, and social interactions. Teachers have a history of seeing how smart he is and using it as the sole measure of his academic capability, not giving any weight or credence to his ADHD, autism, and learning disabilities at all. This adds an enormous amount of stress and anxiety to Ricochet, and crisis behaviors have been common, including school refusal, frequent calls home, and even self-harm at school last year. Because expectations exceeded capability, he and I struggled far beyond what I thought possible. There were times when he tried to exit my vehicle while it was still moving before we reached school drop-off. There were times when administration had to physically take him from my car and escort him into school. There were dozens of days I could not get him to even leave the house.

In contrast, Ricochet now has teachers and administrators at a new school who are open to discovering, listening to, and accepting *his truth*. They accept his weaknesses and support them. They see that he's a smart, wonderful kid who also has challenges. They accept that my insights into his special needs matter. They work with him whenever something is bothering him rather than dismissing his thoughts and feelings. Now, Ricochet goes to school every day willingly and happily. When he comes home, he is still happy. He's literally like a new child, all because the individuals in his life are finally listening to *his truth*.

Your child can be successful and happy, too, despite ADHD, with this parenting approach. Discover your child's truth!

Your Child's True Potential

Now you have a glimpse of what it's like to grow up with ADHD and what that's like for your child. You know that celebrating successes, nurturing talents and interests, and teaching lagging skills are really important. You recognize that grades, popularity, and group activities like athletics aren't that important. And you've learned that the one most crucial ingredient in effectively raising a child with ADHD is to *discover, listen to, and accept your child's truth*. This formula will guide you and your child through defining and achieving their true potential.

All that's left are the skills and opportunities that create success: determination, self-advocacy, using creativity as an advantage, and interest and opportunities from parents and care-givers.

Teach Determination

In 2007, psychologists Duckworth, Peterson, Matthews, and Kelly, set out to discover why some individuals succeed more than others. They found that grit — defined as perseverance/determination and passion for long-term goals — was the essential ingredient in success, not intelligence as many would assume. Their study, published in the *Journal of Personality and Social Psychology*, shows that the intensity at which one pursues their goals is what counts,[xxvi] and kids with ADHD often have a lot of intensity.

Determination is the perseverance that will carry our kids with ADHD over, around, and through obstacles until they achieve success. The ADHD traits of hyperfocus and stubbornness can be redirected to fuel determination. Their uncanny knack for never accepting "no" as an answer to anything is part of that determination that will keep them pushing through.

Many think you are born with determination or not, but I think determination is a skill that can be taught. Modeling behavior is a powerful tool for kids with ADHD because it's so visual. Let your kids watch you struggle and work diligently at something until you eventually succeed. I hope that my kids took away a lesson in determination as they watched me struggle and keep working hard to write and publish my books. They certainly saw me cry that it's too hard, perseverate over bumps in the road such as sales slumps, and succeed with books and awards in hand in the end. I didn't set out to teach a lesson in determination when I decided to write books on ADHD and autism, but the process certainly turned out to be one.

You might model determination for your child in the kitchen, modifying the recipe and baking apple pie after apple pie until you achieve the beautiful and tasty pie you were after. Or pruning and feeding your wilting rose bush week after week until it's covered in prize-worthy blooms again. Maybe you take up running and keep a log showing that you are able to run farther and longer over time by sticking with it and not giving up. Our lives are filled with opportunities to model success through perseverance for our children.

Next, be sure you are acknowledging and praising your child's effort more than the outcome. Praise the fact that your child tried again and again and did not give up, even when they don't succeed. This will show your kids that the work they put into something matters as much, if not more than, the outcome.

This is a hard one for parents of kids who struggle (including me), but don't shelter your child from difficult situations. Place them in situations that will be a challenge — don't choose something so difficult that they can't succeed, but choose something where they will have to stick with it and keep trying in order to succeed. This gives them opportunities to prove to themselves that they can achieve with perseverance. And the message that they can succeed is powerful, since it isn't easy to come by for kids with ADHD.

Tell your child stories about individuals who reached success only after many failures, such as Ben Franklin, Thomas Edison, Jay-Z, Michael Jordan, Walt Disney, or *The Little Engine that Could*.

Don't let your child be a quitter. It's natural for kids with ADHD to want to stop doing something that makes them feel like a failure. It's important to show them the benefit of seeing it through, even if it's painful. Of course, there are situations when quitting is the right thing to do, but encourage your child to persevere and praise their seeing activities and commitments through. In the end, tell your child, "I bet you are really proud of yourself for sticking with it and making it to the end. How does it feel?" You're teaching determination, but also boosting their self-esteem.

Teach Self-Advocacy

Kids with ADHD learn and interact with their environment differently. They need a lot of help and accommodation from others, especially when they are young. Parents can't advocate for a special needs child all their lives, so it's crucial that kids with ADHD and learning disabilities learn to advocate for themselves. Self-advocacy is essentially learning how to express one's own needs.

Since kids don't like being different from their peers, they often don't ask for help and fail to communicate their needs, so this is a skill parents and teachers must teach. Starting at an early age, maybe around third grade or so, will ensure that they are prepared to advocate for their needs on their own by the time they get to college or enter the workforce, where they will be the only ones who can advocate for them.

The first step is to let your child know that it's OK to need help with something. Needing help doesn't make them "stupid" or "inferior." Terry Matlen seconded this notion saying, "Teach your child self-advocacy by teaching them that it's OK to ask teachers for help."

Have their teachers reiterate to them that they won't get upset with any student who asks questions or asks for help — this is a common fear kids have that needs to be addressed openly. If they are embarrassed to raise their hand and ask for help in front of the class, request that the teacher work with your child to create a hand signal that means they need help or need to talk to the teacher privately. I can't tell you how often my kids have come home with bad grades, explained by the fact that they didn't understand the material but were too afraid of potential judgment if they requested help. Be sure to discuss the difference between a must-have and a want.

Advocacy is about asking for what you *need* to even the playing field and have an opportunity to achieve success.

I have Ricochet (with my help) write a letter to his new teachers at the start of each new school year and give it to them at Meet the Teacher/Orientation before school starts. He lists his strengths and interests and shares what he's looking forward to about the new school year, that class, or that teacher. Then he has one paragraph describing what he will need his teachers' help with. It's a low-key way to introduce that Ricochet has special needs right at the outset, and it is usually more openly received since it comes from him, in his own words. It's also a great self-advocacy practice.

Model how to be a good advocate. When advocating for your child, make sure they witness it (at least the positive aspects, not the fighting tooth-and-nail to get the accommodation). Use phrases like, "My child is struggling to <u>concentrate and focus on his seatwork during class</u>. Can he <u>have headphones or sit in a quiet corner of the classroom to do his individual work</u>?" This illustrates for your child that they need to (1) state the struggle they're having and, (2) offer a solution that will be helpful to them. If your child doesn't have a lot of self-awareness yet and/or doesn't know what might help with a particular struggle, talk through identifying the issue, brainstorming potential causes, and problem-solving with them to strengthen those skills, as they are crucial to the self-advocacy process.

Ideally, your child would attend IEP or 504 Plan meetings with you to see firsthand how the advocacy process works for students with special needs. However, you should consider this very carefully. These meetings are often very contentious and focus too heavily on the student's weaknesses, which will only make your child feel worse about themselves and squash any faith that the process works.

I took Ricochet to a school team meeting with me in fourth grade, and it was disastrous. He was furious about all the negative things being said about him and by how little understanding his teachers had of him. I waited until the end of sixth grade, when the school's misinformed opinion of him had reached a boiling point, before I had him attend another IEP meeting. That time, I had him do a typing tutorial on the computer while wearing headphones until after everyone had voiced their complaints, argued with me relentlessly, and were ready to hear what Ricochet thought would help him in school. That helped to prevent his self-esteem from further damage.

Modeling, support, and practice are the key ingredients to teaching your child effective self-advocacy skills.

"At first [my parents] advocated for me, then they taught me to advocate for myself. This skill has served me well throughout my life," offered Leslie. Exactly!

Use Strengths to Overcome Weakness

All human beings have strengths and weaknesses. It just so happens that individuals with ADHD have a specific set of weaknesses that can be very challenging in school and in life, which often makes their weaknesses much more evident. Avoiding things you're not good at can hold you back. The key is to use one's strengths to overcome their weaknesses instead.

To match an individual's strengths with weaknesses to use them in this way, start by making a list of your child's strengths and weaknesses. Since this is an activity designed to teach a skill, get your child involved and ask them to help you draft the list. Make sure you list more strengths than weaknesses to keep this lesson positive. Once you have a list of strengths in one column and weaknesses in a column beside it, start matching strengths and weaknesses. Identify which strength can help with each weakness. Here's an example pairing:

Weakness	Matching Strength
Unfocused, easily distracted	Pair it with one of your child's interests
Impulsive	Ready to try new things
Hyperactive/Restless	Energetic
Hyperfocus	Determined/Persistent
Not good at writing	Great at drawing or shooting photos or video
Takes risks	Creativity and thinking outside the box

In sixth grade, Ricochet had a social studies project on Greek history. There were lots of options for this project, and Ricochet knew not to choose an option that required an essay. Instead, he chose to build a model of a Greek chariot. When he came home, showed me the options, and told me what he had chosen, I cringed. This particular option required drawing blueprints and making a chariot that actually rolled. Due to dysgraphia, he cannot draw accurately. And he tends to rush through tasks and throw his hands up in frustration if it doesn't work out on the first attempt. I felt ninety-nine percent certain he couldn't succeed with this project option. I tried to talk him into easier projects, such as bringing in Greek food products, but he wouldn't hear of it. He wanted to make the chariot because it meant doing some woodworking with his daddy.

Ah-ha! He wanted to use his interests and aptitudes to get this done. What a great plan! He had the right idea all along, and I was late to the party. Ricochet was pushing his dad to work on the project every weekend, instead of the other way around, because he was interested in and excited about woodworking. He used his strength in doing hands-on projects and creativity to overcome the challenges of a long-term school project. *Way to go, Bud!*

Is it possible to negate and overcome every weakness? Of course not. We also have to learn to rely on our strengths and not get caught up in our weaknesses. I have some fairly extreme anxiety, especially socially. It would be unwise for me to take a job as the public face of a company or interviewing people on television. There's no way I could succeed at that. Instead, I looked at my passion for conveying a message and my strength in the written word and paired them to become a writer. It's a way to get my stories, and those of others, out without challenging my weaknesses to a breaking point. No one can be good at everything. Part of using strengths to overcome weaknesses is knowing in which direction to steer yourself.

"I think my aunt encouraging me by taking me to drama and theatre is what helped get me though middle school and high school because it gave me a purpose outside that horrible place. She knew I cared about acting so much that she would drive through really bad snowy road conditions to get me to rehearsals," shared Marlow.

"Help [your child] learn who they are, what limits to set for themselves, and, most important, help them embrace the unique brain they have been given to see the world differently," Bonnie wrote. "These are the kids who will change the world if only given a chance." Indeed!

Take an Interest

Spending quality time with your kids offers so many rewards. First, it gives you extra opportunities to model appropriate behaviors like self-awareness, social skills, and frustration tolerance, to name a few. In addition, kids whose parents take an interest in their lives and spend quality time with them are often better adjusted, more successful in school, and participate less in risky behaviors. Remember, kids who crave adult attention but don't get it are more likely to act out in order to ensure the attention they desire.

When parents ask about their lives, encourage their interests, give good advice, and spend free time with them in school activities, teens have fewer behavioral problems.[xxvii] Leisure activities as a family, even those as simple as watching TV together or playing board games, have been found to directly correlate to the ability to adapt.[xxviii] Children's academic success has been linked to moms talking to and listing to their children.[xxix] Preteens and teens receive better grades when their fathers spend time with them inside and outside the home than kids whose fathers don't spend quality time with them.[xxx]

Spending time together also strengthens family bonds. It shows your child that you love them, value them, and are there for them. Spending time with your child also shows them that you are dependable and can be trusted.

Of course, you learn more about your child the more time you spend with them — a key ingredient to successfully raising a child with ADHD.

Offer Opportunities for Success

Kids with ADHD tend to have low self-esteem because they're in a world that has some everyday expectations out of their reach. They are bombarded with failures but have few opportunities for successes on their own, especially in school. As they experience more and more successes, your child's self-esteem and confidence will build.

Allocate time to nurture your child's talents and interests to offer opportunities for success. Cultivate your child's talents and interests together, and you'll reap the rewards of spending time with your child, as well as offer them the gratification of success.

Talents and interests aren't the only areas that offer successes for kids with ADHD. Parents must craft an environment for their kids that offers everyday successes as well. The most important element is setting appropriate expectations for your child, in light of their ADHD. Remember, ADHD is a developmental disability, meaning your child is two to three years behind their peers developmentally, socially, emotionally, and cognitively. If expectations are beyond a child's reach, they cannot succeed, no matter how hard they try. Make sure your expectations at home, as well as the expectations set upon them at school, are developmentally appropriate so they have opportunities for success.

"Even though I struggled with academics," Hannah shared, "I was able to feel successful by spending a lot of time doing what I excelled in."

Lynn shares the same story, "My horrible middle and high school grades, and even mediocre college grades, made no difference in my adult life. I created my own success, which is something typical of [individuals with ADHD]. When I was ready, I was ready."

The more opportunities for success your child experiences, the better their self-esteem and confidence will be, setting them up for success down the road.

**

Help your child discover *their* truth, accept and listen to their truth, and give them the skills and opportunities to succeed. As the adults with ADHD have shown us, that's the most important formula to raise happy, successful kids who happen to have ADHD.

Thank you for reading!

Dear Reader,

I hope you enjoyed *The Insider's Guide to ADHD: Adults with ADHD Reveal the Secret to Parenting Kids with ADHD*. Writing this book has been both enlightening and rewarding. For updates on my special boy, as well as more information on parenting kids with ADHD, follow my blog at ParentingADHDandAutism.com or BoyWithoutInstructions.com.

I receive numerous emails from blog readers and readers of my other books thanking me for sharing our journey and compiling ADHD resources. As an author, I love feedback, so that is very rewarding. You and your family are the reason I will continue to write about ADHD. So, tell me what you liked, what you loved, and even what you hated about this book. I would truly love to hear from you. Write to me at penny@pennywilliamsauthor.com and visit me online at ParentingADHDandAutism.com.

I need to ask a favor. I'd love a review of *The Insider's Guide to ADHD*. Positive or negative, I need your feedback. Reviews are tough to come by, but they can make or break the success of a book and its author. If you can spare just five minutes, please visit the *Insider's Guide* pages on Amazon.com and Goodreads.com and submit your candid review.

Thank you for reading The *Insider's Guide to ADHD* and riding along on my journey. Look for my other books, *Boy Without Instructions* and *What to Expect When Parenting Children with ADHD*.

With sincerest gratitude,
Penny Williams

Appendix

Appendix A: The Adult ADHD Survey

Below is the survey I used to gather a great deal of the data offered in this book.

ADHD Adult Survey: Advice for Parents of Kids w/ ADHD

Thank you for taking the time to complete this survey about your ADHD. I am working on research for my 3rd book, a compilation of advice for parents of children with ADHD from adults who grew up struggling with ADHD. Your answers should be for your entire childhood, up to 18 years of age. If you feel a question is not applicable, please use the "other" option to give that answer.

What is your gender? *
- o   Male
- o   Female

What is your current age? *
- o   Under 15
- o   15 to 17
- o   18 to 24
- o   25 to 34
- o   35 to 44
- o   45 to 54
- o   55 to 64
- o   65 to 74
- o   75 or older

At what age were you diagnosed with ADHD? *
- o   4-5
- o   6-7
- o   8-10
- o   11-13
- o   14-16
- o   16-20
- o   20s
- o   30s
- o   40s
- o   50s
- o   60s
- o   70 or older

At what age did you start taking medication?*

- o I never took ADHD medication.
- o 4-5
- o 6-7
- o 8-10
- o 11-13
- o 14-16
- o 16-20
- o 20s
- o 30s
- o 40s
- o 50s
- o 60s
- o 70 or older

How did you do in school (elementary, middle, and high school) as a child?*

- o did well. I was able to get good grades without too much struggle.
- o I had to work really hard, but I got A's and B's on my report cards.
- o School was a struggle. I got by though.
- o School was a disaster. My grades were atrocious.
- o School was the worst. My grades were poor, and I was always in trouble.
- o Other:

The best / most helpful thing my parents did for me as a child (as it relates to my ADHD) was...*

The best / most helpful thing a teacher did for me as a child (as it relates to my ADHD) was...*

What advice would you give to parents raising kids with ADHD? Something you wish your parents or teachers did? Something you wish you did for yourself? Etc...*

Please leave me your name, phone, and email if you are open to being contacted for further interview for my research. You can participate anonymously. There will definitely be more questions to clarify information

Based on your personal childhood experience, rate each of the following on importance for parents to focus on when raising a child with ADHD *

	Not high on my priority list.	It matters, but many other things are more important.	Important, but some other things are more important.	Very, very important!	N/A
Focus/attention skills	○	○	○	○	○
Impulsivity and thinking before acting	○	○	○	○	○
Academic performance overall	○	○	○	○	○
Grades	○	○	○	○	○
Self-Esteem	○	○	○	○	○
Having lots of friends	○	○	○	○	○
Having close friends	○	○	○	○	○
Playing sports	○	○	○	○	○
Getting regular exercise	○	○	○	○	○
Nurturing a talent or interest	○	○	○	○	○

Rate the following sources of motivation when you were a child with ADHD. *

	This was a huge motivator! Motivated me every time!	This helped to motivate me.	This didn't make a difference one way or the other -- didn't motivate me, nor demotivate me.	This was a real downer -- often made me less motivated rather than more.	N/A
My own desire to do well	○	○	○	○	○
Praise from teachers	○	○	○	○	○
Punishment from teachers	○	○	○	○	○
Being shamed by teachers	○	○	○	○	○
Praise from parents/family	○	○	○	○	○
Punishment from parents/family	○	○	○	○	○
Being shamed by parents/family	○	○	○	○	○
Being made to feel guilty by elders	○	○	○	○	○

	This was a huge motivator! Motivated me every time!	This helped to motivate me.	This didn't make a difference one way or the other -- didn't motivate me, nor demotivate me.	This was a real downer -- often made me less motivated rather than more.	N/A
Being made fun of by peers	○	○	○	○	○
Being ostracized by peers	○	○	○	○	○
ADHD medication	○	○	○	○	○
Help from therapist and/or coach	○	○	○	○	○
Teacher believing in me	○	○	○	○	○
Parents believing in me	○	○	○	○	○
Coach believing in me	○	○	○	○	○

	This was a huge motivator! Motivated me every time!	This helped to motivate me.	This didn't make a difference one way or the other -- didn't motivate me, nor demotivate me.	This was a real downer -- often made me less motivated rather than more.	N/A
Support of my church	○	○	○	○	○
Support of other community member	○	○	○	○	○

What strategies did you find most helpful in your day-to-day as a child with ADHD? *

- ○ Parent helping me manage every little thing (overseeing homework, packing backpack, etc.)
- ○ Wrote everything in a planner
- ○ Used technology and reminder alerts
- ○ Left myself notes all over the place (Post-It notes maybe)
- ○ Parent left me notes but didn't nag
- ○ Getting everything in writing
- ○ Getting space and time to cool off and pull things together on my own
- ○ Asking for help
- ○ Other:

What do you feel was the biggest help to your self-esteem and confidence as a child? *

- O Participating in activities I liked and/or was good at.
- O Positive feedback and praise from my parents consistently.
- O Positive feedback and praise from teachers consistently.
- O Having lots of friends.
- O Having really close friends/a best friend.
- O Being popular in school.
- O Being good at a sport.
- O Succeeding in school by getting good grades.
- O Other:

Appendix B: The Adults Who Were Quoted in the Book

Terry Matlen
Age 55-64
Diagnosed in her 40s

Ella
Age 25-34
Diagnosed at 11-13

Lynn
Age 35-44
Diagnosed in her 40s

Rachel
Age 45-54
Diagnosed in her 40s

Anne
Age 45-54
Diagnosed in her 50s

Jessica
Age 35-44
Diagnosed in her 30s

Samantha
Age 55-64
Diagnosed in her 40s

Naomi
Age 55-64
Diagnosed in her 50s

Leslie
Age 25-34
Diagnosed at age 4 or 5

Eva
Age 25-34
Diagnosed in her 30s

Keith
Age 35-44
Diagnosed between the ages of 8-10

Carson
Age 25-34
Diagnosed at the age of 4 or 5

Wanda
Age 45-54
Diagnosed in her 40s

Frannie
Age 18-24
Diagnosed between the ages of 8-10

Marlow
Age 18-24
Diagnosed in her 20s

Martin
Age 25-34
Diagnosed at age 6 or 7

Joyce
Age 45-54
Diagnosed in her 30's

Colleen
Age 65-74
Diagnosed in her 50s

Maggie
Age 45-54
Diagnosed in her 30s

Ingrid
Age 35-44
Diagnosed in her 30s

Mary
Age 35-44
Diagnosed in her 40s

Mark
Age 65-74
Diagnosed in his 50s

Melissa
Age 55-64
Diagnosed in her 50s

Jake
Age 35-44
Diagnosed in his 40s

Brent
Age 45-54
Diagnosed at the age of
6 or 7

Stephanie
Age 35-44
Diagnosed in her 40s

Joanie
Age 35-44
Diagnosed in her 30s

Marshall
Age 45-54
Diagnosed in his 20s

Samuel
Age 35-44
Diagnosed in his 20s

Dorothy
Age 65-74
Diagnosed in her 50s

Anabelle
Age 35-44
Diagnosed in her 20s

Susan
Age 18-24
Diagnosed between the
ages of 11-13

Kate
Age 35-44
Diagnosed in her 40s

Leslie
Age 25-34
Diagnosed between the
ages of 16-20

Kerri
Age 18-24
Diagnosed between the
ages of 8-10

Nicole
Age 35-44
Diagnosed in her 20s

Bonnie
Age 35-44
Diagnosed in her 30s

Diana
Age 35-44
Diagnosed in her 30s

Ralph
Age 45-54
Diagnosed at the age of
6 or 7

Evelyn
Age 25-34
Diagnosed at the age of
6 or 7

Scott
Age 18-24
Diagnosed between the
ages of 11-13

Cooper
Age 25-34
Diagnosed in his 20s

Alyssa
Age 14
Diagnosed between the
ages of 8-10

Hannah
Age 35-44
Diagnosed between the
ages of 14-16

Audrey
Age 18-24
Diagnosed between the
ages of 16-20

Lillian
Age 35-44
Diagnosed in her 40s

Larry
Age 18-24
Diagnosed between the
ages of 11-13

Caroline
Age 35-44
Diagnosed between the
ages of 8-10

Endnotes

i. "What Is Attention Deficit Hyperactivity Disorder (ADHD)?" NIMH RSS. US Department of Health and Human Services, n.d. Web. 11 Feb. 2015.

ii. "About SPD - SPD and Other Disorders." SPD Foundation - About SPD - SPD and Other Disorders. SPD Foundation, n.d. Web. 11 Mar. 2015.

iii. Cheung PP, Siu AM. A comparison of patterns of sensory processing in children with and without developmental disabilities. Res Dev Disabil. 2009;30:1468–1480.

iv. Dunn W, Bennett D. Patterns of sensory processing in children with attention deficit hyperactivity disorder. Occup Ther J Res. 2002;22:4–15.

v. Ghanizadeh A.Sensory Processing Problems in Children with ADHD, a Systematic Review.Psychiatry Investig. 2011 Jun;8(2):89-94.http://dx.doi.org/10.4306/pi.2011.8.2.89

vi. Dunn W, Bennett D. Patterns of sensory processing in children with attention deficit hyperactivity disorder. Occup Ther J Res. 2002;22:4–15.

vii. Dodson, William W., MD. "Real-World Office Management of ADHD in Adults." Real-World Office Management of ADHD in Adults. Psychiatric Times, 1 Nov. 2006. Web. 11 Mar. 2015.

viii. Attention Deficit Hyperactivity Disorder." NIMH. National Institutes of Health, 2012. Web. 05 Oct. 2015.

ix. Attention Deficit Hyperactivity Disorder." NIMH. National Institutes of Health, 2012. Web. 05 Oct. 2015.

x. Kessler RC, Adler L, Barkley R, Biederman J, Conners CK, Demler O, Faraone SV, Greenhill LL, Howes MJ, Secnik K, Spencer T, Ustun TB, Walters EE, Zaslavsky AM.American Journal of Psychiatry. 2006. 163: 724-732.

xi.   "Stimulant ADHD Medications: Methylphenidate and Amphetamines."DrugFacts. National Institutes of Health, Jan. 2014. Web. 05 Oct. 2015.

xii.   Attention Deficit Hyperactivity Disorder." NIMH. National Institutes of Health, 2012. Web. 05 Oct. 2015.

xiii. Young, Karen. "Toxic People Affect Kids Too." Hey Sigmund. N.p., 26 May 2015. Web. 05 Oct. 2015.

xiv.   Loader, P. (1998), Such a shame—a consideration of shame and shaming mechanisms in families. Child Abuse Rev., 7: 44–57. doi: 10.1002/(SICI)1099-0852(199801/02)7:1<44::AID-CAR334>3.0.CO;2-7

xv.   Review of Child Development Research, Volume 1, edited by Lois Wladis Hoffman, Martin L. Hoffman

xvi.   Aunola, K., Tolvanen, A., Viljaranta, J. & Nurmi, J.-E.. Psychological control in daily parent-child interactions increases children's negative emotions. Journal of Family Psychology. 2013

xvii. Belden AC, Barch DM, Oakberg TJ, et al. Anterior Insula Volume and Guilt: Neurobehavioral Markers of Recurrence After Early Childhood Major Depressive Disorder. JAMA Psychiatry. 2015;72(1):40-48. doi:10.1001/jamapsychiatry.2014.1604.

xviii. How many friends does one person need?" Dunbar, R. 2010, Faber & Faber, London.

xix.   Demir, Melikşah, Metin Özdemir, and Lesley A. Weitekamp. "Looking to Happy Tomorrows with Friends: Best and Close Friendships as They Predict Happiness." Journal of Happiness Studies 8.2 (2007): 243-71.

xx.   Demır, Melıkşah, and Lesley A. Weitekamp. "I Am so Happy 'Cause Today I Found My Friend: Friendship and Personality as Predictors of Happiness." Journal of Happiness Studies 8.2 (2007): 181-211. Web.

xxi.   "Psychological and Social Benefits of Playing True Sport." TrueSport. U.S. Anti-Doping Agency, 2014. Web. 05 Oct. 2015.

xxii. Dodson, William W., MD. "Real-World Office Management of ADHD in Adults." Real-World Office Management of ADHD in Adults. Psychiatric Times, 1 Nov. 2006. Web. 11 Mar. 2015.

xxiii. Bernstein, Jeffery, Ph.D. "Five Easy, Powerful Ways to Validate Your Child's Feelings." Psychology Today. Sussex Publishers, LLC, 20 Sept. 2013. Web. 04 Apr. 2015.

xxiv. Robert H. Bradley, Bettye M. Caldwell and Stephen L. Rock. "Home Environment and School Performance: A Ten-Year Follow-Up and Examination of Three Models of Environmental Action." Child Development. Vol. 59, No. 4 (Aug., 1988) , pp. 852-867

xxv. Johnston, Craig A., Chermaine Tyler, Sandra A. Stansberry, Jennette P. Moreno, and John P. Foreyt. "Brief Report: Gum Chewing Affects Standardized Math Scores in Adolescents." Journal of Adolescence35.2 (2012): 455-59. Web.

xxvi. Duckworth, A.L., Peterson, C., Matthews, M.D., & Kelly, D.R. (2007). Grit: Perseverance and passion for long-term goals. Journal of Personality and Social Psychology, 9, 1087-1101.

xxvii. Michelle J. Pearce, "The Protective Effects of Religiousness and Parent Involvement on the Development of Conduct Problems Among Youth Exposed to Violence," Child Development 74, No. 6 (November/December 2003): 1682-1696

xxviii. Ramon B. Zabriskie, and Bryan P. McCormick, "The Influences of Family Leisure Patterns on Perceptions of Family Functioning," Family Relations 50, No. 3 (July 2001): 281-289.

xxix. Tom Luster et al., "Family Advocates' Perspectives on the Early Academic Success of Children Born to Low-Income Adolescent Mothers," Family Relations 53, No. 1 (January 2004): 68-77.

xxx. Elizabeth C. Cooksey and Michelle M. Fondell, "Spending Time with His Kids: Effects of Family Structure on Fathers' and Children's Lives," Journal of Marriage and the Family 58 (August 1996): 693-707.

Get more guidance and mentoring with Penny Williams, a.k.a., the ADHD Momma!

What to Expect When Parenting Children with ADHD

The contrast between expectations and genuine capability is stark but invisible with ADHD, creating challenges every moment in all aspects of life. Use *What to Expect* and the 25+ worksheets included to learn about your child's behaviors, triggers, strengths, and weaknesses, to improve life for your child with ADHD, and your entire family.

Boy Without Instructions

Right before your eyes, this initially grief-stricken momma transforms from obsessed-with-ADHD control-freak and helicopter mom to optimistic and (mostly) confident parent of a child who happens to have ADHD. *Boy Without Instructions* validates your grief and guilt, yet reveals that it's truly possible to craft a (mostly) joy-filled life for your family.

Purchase Penny's other titles on Amazon.com, BarnesandNoble.com, and through other select retailers.

ONLINE COURSES

Penny's online school, the **Parenting ADHD & Autism Academy**, offers online training for challenged parents. The courses guide and mentor parents raising kids with ADHD and/or high-functioning autism. Penny teaches you where to start when diagnosed, parenting strategies specific to ADHD and autism, behavior modification, how to work with schools, parent self-care, setting your child up for success, and much more. Visit the academy at **ParentingADHDandAutismAcademy. com** to learn more and register for courses.

WEBSITE

Visit **ParentingADHDandAutism.com** for effective tips and strategies in several formats: articles, sharing quality resources, how-to videos, online courses, and parent coaching.